OFF THE
GRID

OFF THE
GRID

MY RIDE FROM LOUISIANA TO THE PANAMA CANAL IN AN ELECTRIC CAR

RANDY DENMON

Foreword by Jim Motavalli

Skyhorse Publishing

Skyhorse Publishing books may be purchased in bulk at special discounts for sales promotion, corporate gifts, fund-raising, or educational purposes. Special editions can also be created to specifications. For details, contact the Special Sales Department, Skyhorse Publishing, 307 West 36th Street, 11th Floor, New York, NY 10018 or info@skyhorsepublishing.com.

Skyhorse® and Skyhorse Publishing® are registered trademarks of Skyhorse Publishing, Inc.®, a Delaware corporation.

Visit our website at www.skyhorsepublishing.com.

10 9 8 7 6 5 4 3 2 1

Library of Congress Cataloging-in-Publication Data is available on file.

Cover design by Rain Saukas
Cover photo credit: iStock

Print ISBN: 978-1-5107-1739-8
Ebook ISBN: 978-1-5107-1740-4

Printed in the United States of America

Men wanted for hazardous journey to the South Pole. Small wages, bitter cold, long months of complete darkness, constant danger. Safe return doubtful. Honor and recognition in case of success.

—Ad placed in a London paper by Ernest Shackleton for his 1902 Discovery Expedition. He said later: "So overwhelming was the response to his appeal that it seemed as though all the men of Great Britain were determined to accompany him."

Contents

Foreword

Asked why they bought an SUV when a sedan or minivan made more sense, many Americans cite the concept of "personal freedom," meaning that—if they wanted to—they could take it off road, into the trackless wilderness and fordable streams featured in the commercials. Of course, only 15 percent of owners actually take their SUVs off the school/work/mall/house-of-worship axis, but it's important to these buyers to know they could.

Four-wheel-drive boxes are dominating the market, while battery electrics are in the doldrums—only .37 percent of the American market in 2016. Why? Price and range anxiety mostly, though that's changing as affordable 200-mile cars like the Chevy Bolt hit the market.

The Tesla Model S, the car owned by *Off the Grid* author Randy Denmon, can travel up to 265 miles on a charge. And that means owners rarely suffer range anxiety, and they can—and do—take their cars across country, or at least on long vacations. You meet Teslas in the craziest places these days.

There are 790 Tesla Supercharger stations in the United States, and what a comfort that is for travel in the Lower 48. But somebody had to be the trailblazer to take their Tesla further afield, and that turns out to be Randy Denmon, with his complaining sidekick Dean Lewis.

In the grand tradition of Don Quixote and Sancho Panza, or more recently Bill Bryson and Stephen Katz taking a walk in the woods, they leave the Superchargers behind at the Mexican border and head due south—with the Panama Canal as their destination. And bicker with each other the whole way.

Like *Fear and Loathing in Las Vegas*—without the drugs, but with the paranoia—this is a road book and a rollicking adventure story. It's called *Off the Grid*, but actually it's *about* the grid, or at least the patched-together, intermittently available version of it that exists south of the border.

Will our intrepid heroes connect to 230 volts before their battery indicator reads zero and they're stranded in the middle of nowhere, waiting for the drug cartels to swoop down? Will the Tesla survive potholed roads, torrential storms and crooked customs officials with their hands out for bribes?

You'll have to read the book to find out, but there's no doubt that even attempting a crazy trip like this is a sign that electric cars are—finally—entering the mainstream. And you bet that's a good thing.

Jim Motavalli
Fairfield, CT
January 2017

We're Off

Under a sapphire sky, the guard post on the south abutment of the three-mile long Anzalduas International Bridge came into view. Below, in a deep gorge, the Rio Grande trickled by, an unassuming brown slice of water. The far bank seemed no different from McAllen, Texas, a multitude of concrete and buildings wedged between throngs of people.

But on the other side, *everything* was different. The land was foreign and exotic, the people mysterious. Over there, nothing back here mattered. The little river divided two peoples, one born into a fortunate land, the others. . . .

The federal agents of the United Mexican States stood in their imposing uniforms, machine guns held at port arms. The cool January morning was clear, temperature in the forties, and a half-moon was setting to the west.

Where were we going? Butterflies filled my stomach. My hands twitched.

I have heard all journeys have a purpose, even directionless ones. This journey had a direction, if little else. Maybe it was a spiritual trip as much as a physical journey.

The queue of cars inched forward. I turned to Dean Lewis as I eased the wonderful piece of modern technology that would get us across the border, just a few feet in front of us. The four-door sedan looked rather plain, like something any typical American salesman or soccer mom would employ to efficiently move through suburbia. But this high-tech machine, the new Tesla Model S, was powered only by electricity.

Two Louisiana rednecks were fixing to drive this car through Latin America to Panama, and maybe beyond. Perhaps not my brightest idea, but then, I have been known to pursue some insane endeavors.

The EPA estimates the range of this Tesla at 265 miles per charge. Of course, that's running at a constant 65 mph, with no air conditioning, with only 300 pounds of cargo, over flat ground, without headwind, and without other devices—wipers, lights, radio, etc. Who knew what the real-world range of the car would be over bumpy, third-world roads, crossing varied terrain loaded down with 600 or 700 pounds of cargo? Theoretically, the car could travel over 400 miles at a constant speed of 35 mph. But then, everything works in theory, or over a smooth test track somewhere in California.

I looked to the dash and the car's speed-range curve. Bigger problems lay ahead other than the car's range, most notably, how would we charge the vehicle's lithium-ion battery pack every day? It takes twelve hours to charge the Tesla with standard 240-volt, 30-amp power, and two and a half days with 120-volt electricity, equivalent to a two-prong plug for a typical American living-room lamp.

I had conjured up the idea of this trip a year before, really only hoping I might get a chance to give it a go in the near future. Maybe the trip would produce a book? We'd see how it all turned out.

I had, over the last year, learned how to get a Tesla charged in rural Louisiana. Two factors were critical: 1) have plenty of charging cords—the power source might be a significant distance from the pavement, and 2) have plenty of charging options. In the United States, there are more than twenty-five available sockets that supply 240-volt power.

Before the trip, I fabricated two very long 240-volt extension cords with a combined length of three hundred feet. These are big, thick rolls of three-quarter-inch wire that weigh about thirty pounds each. I had also purchased all the plugs and adapters I could get my hands on.

As for driving through Mexico and Central America, I did very little planning. It's kind of like driving across America. Of course, there are a few small differences. It's too dangerous to drive at night, and the roads are much worse or likely to be closed without warning, and you've got perpetual military checkpoints, shady cops, and bad guys. You get the picture.

A couple of weeks before we departed, I did research the best route through Mexico, the best route being solely determined by safety and the current status of the Drug War. There were three or four areas that needed to be avoided at all cost, but there's no ducking the bloody, border region south of Texas. What was the best and quickest way through here? I thought I had it. Onward, where to get a charge and how to keep safe on the road would govern the route, and determining that would likely be best determined by word of mouth and day to day.

We had really departed on a whim. I had a rare break in my work schedule. Dean was available and willing. It was now time to get in the car and *GO*.

The third world lay ahead. Charging the car and finding our way would certainly be a difficult, cautious process of trial and error.

• • •

How had I arrived here? Somehow, my life had gotten too boring, plain. It needed spice. Something more than just producing more goods and services than I consumed. What had happened to that young, adventurous, romantic young man who freely passed the days doing nothing, smiling, enjoying almost anything, even a trip to the grocery or just a beautiful spring day?

Surely, like many urban American men of my age, in the prime of their lives, I wasn't starting to suffer from that awful disease—having such a vastly inflated opinion of one's self-worth that my disappearance for just a few weeks would result in a national disaster or cause the Earth to stop spinning. Still, I needed something—adventure, freedom. Maybe this—especially if we succeeded—would appease my trampled, wandering spirit before I looked into the mirror and saw nothing but a nerdy, yuppie robot.

Somehow my life had been transformed into a daily grind of bland social outings and long hours at the office, all without zest. Now in my forties, I seemed to move through the world without meaning or direction. Nothing made the soul explode with anxiety or joy as it did in my youthful days, when optimism penetrated everything. I needed to get off the grid, away from the cell phones and emails. I needed some freedom. An overreaction? For sure it would be a hell of an undertaking, worthy of headlines.

Just a few days earlier, the national papers had been filled with stories of the first cross-country trip in an electric car, Los Angeles to New York. That was peanuts compared to what we were attempting. A few electric vehicle (EV) enthusiasts had plans to drive to Alaska, and message boards across the country were filled with threads discussing how to drive an electric car across rural

Wyoming or Texas. But nobody had yet attempted anything this bold. Even if we failed, just trying would soothe my psyche. We had the balls to try if nothing else.

• • •

I reached to the backseat and grabbed a pack of cigarettes, throwing it on the dash.

Dean looked at me, his forehead crinkled. "You're not going to smoke those all the way there, are you?"

"I'm only a recreational smoker," I said as I lit up, exhaling a long drag to calm my nerves. "I'm trying to take up Nicorette gum, but it's costing me a fortune. Not from the price of the gum, but the two root canals I needed from chewing on that shit. But my experience has been, in Mexico, and probably everywhere else we're going, American cigarettes seem to appease the local bureaucrats."

"Just give them the pack then. Save your lungs."

"Giving them a pack of cigarettes might be construed as bribery. Having a smoke with them, and accidentally leaving a pack is just good foreign relations and forgetfulness."

I pulled up to the Mexican Customs and Immigration building. We had to get our driving permits and bond the car to get it across the border, in addition to our passports.

Another long drag, and the nicotine shot through my synapses. The last two days had been hectic. I had no idea what the coming ones would bring, or the magnitude of problems and setbacks we'd face.

What could go wrong? For months, my mind had been besieged with endless scenarios that now sped into my brain. A stolen car, a wreck, or mechanical problems were statistically the most likely. The latter two were as problematic as the first because repairing a Tesla in Latin America would be almost impossible.

Could we get such a car across so many borders? Would the primitive roads be too much for the sedan, its clearance only a little over five inches? Would we get stranded in the middle of nowhere, unable to charge? We'd be driving through the murder capital of the world, Honduras, and a few other countries not far behind that statistic. My simple little life was about to enter a realm of chaos.

One Day Earlier

The silver Dodge truck nudged forward atop one of HWY 59's triple-deck overpasses. Ah, Houston congestion. Hardly an open space occupied the thirteen lanes of freeway. I scanned the strip malls and subdivisions outside the window, where the traffic, clustered and snarled, moved along at a snail's pace. It was only 4:30 in the afternoon. What would it look like in thirty minutes or an hour?

I looked around in amazement at the urban jungle. I knew this city well, and its traffic. Over the years, I'd wasted what seemed like years sitting idle on these modern concrete arteries, watching bright red taillights and listening to honking horns. We were now south of Houston and might make the 300 miles to McAllen in time to get some sleep before our early start the next day.

• • •

The day before, I'd left my dizzying world behind. There had been the mundane, personal chores before any extended leave: paying bills, arranging for mail to be picked up, etc. These were rather simple as I'm single and without dependents.

But as a partner in a multimillion-dollar engineering firm, for which I had been named president only a year earlier, larger problems had to be sorted out. There were dozens of projects and clients to keep happy. Needless to say, it was a monumental chore that would require managing, even from half a continent away.

I looked at my desk one last time. Stacks of paper abounded: bills, invoices, drawings, letters, engineering reports of every type. My days were filled with endless meetings and emails. I was a dull workaholic. My profession had been partially responsible for this, if not the catalyst. Engineering is a job with long, mind-numbing days filled with paperwork, deadlines, endless correspondence, staring at a CADD drawing on a computer screen, and worrying about your work. I'd even started to find the task of sending out invoices burdensome. Certainly, I wouldn't miss that world.

Over the years, my friends had become dads, some with kids now in college! A few friends had even passed from this world from natural causes.

Ahead there would be no monotonous meetings to attend, no agonizing decisions of whether to go on an exhausting run or bike ride, no worrying about what to wear, or having to attend the social gatherings to see the same people talk about the same things.

I had decided, at least for a time, to start living again, not in the cookie-cutter box the world had made for us but instead unbound by everyday rules and norms. What I really yearned for—a challenge, the unknown, some true gratification—hopefully lay ahead.

I turned to my computer where I'd typed out an email to some current clients. The missive was carefully vague, stating only that I'd be out of the country on vacation for several weeks, and giving the contact information of others in my office who could lend a hand in my absence. Only a fool would entrust the management of a multimillion-dollar project to someone who would head off where I intended to go. A few recipients might envy me, but most would probably think I was crazy.

I clicked the mouse and sent the message out into cyberspace, almost not believing I was really leaving.

• • •

Now, beside me in the Dodge truck, Dean silently doodled on a computer pad. Fraternity brothers at Louisiana Tech a quarter century prior, we'd both been reared and had spent our formidable years in Louisiana's Mississippi Delta, traipsing the flatlands in the heart of the Protestant South.

Black-headed, with sharp, alert eyes, Dean stands about my height, five feet, ten inches tall. I'm thin and wobbly, but Dean's frame is thick and sturdy. Or at least it used to be sturdy. Like me, a bulging, pudgy ring of tissue had developed around his mid-section in recent years. Dean's life wasn't as rigid as mine. After we'd both served in the Gulf War, the Army had sent him on to the Defense Language Institute to study Chinese. Where he'd gone from there was probably classified. His military days long over, he'd recently returned from working as a business consultant in China for several years. His side of the story was that the pollution in China had chased him back to the land of capitalism and federally mandated environmental laws—which usually means clean water and air. Whatever the truth, he had a break from the real world while he looked for a new career, and the trip fit his meandering nature.

I wasn't really surprised when Dean agreed to take the trip with me. He was well equipped for it, having frequently spent months, if not years, working in some of the world's most exotic locales in the Middle East and Asia. Extremely low maintenance and frugal by nature, strange landscapes didn't frighten him.

Unlike most travelers who go away and think of nothing but home, almost ready to return the day they leave, he liked to wander without the constraints of time.

At least I'd thought he fit the profile until that morning. As we departed, he walked down the stairs of my house carrying two king-sized pillows covered with 300 thread-count cotton cases.

"Do we have room for these?" he asked.

"You gotta be shittin' me," I said. "Where the hell do you think we're going?"

I leaned up from the Dodge's back seat to look at Steve Malloy, a friend of ours with a trucking business who'd agreed to lug us and the Tesla to the border.

Steve flashed his blue eyes at me as he tuned the truck's radio. "I'd love to go with you."

Boy, I bet you would, I thought, knowing his marriage was on the rocks. I said, "You've got your kids and your business." I turned to Steve's driver, Rick. "You two have got a ten-hour drive back to Monroe. Maybe you can give Steve some marital advice to pass the time."

"Not me," Rick said, laughing. "I'm on my fifth wife."

The traffic slowed a tad. I looked out at the maze of people rushing to be somewhere, rats in a race. Strangely, I felt sorry for them. In the car beside us, a middle-aged man talked on the phone. He wore a nice suit and looked the part of a successful professional. How uninspiring. Above, a flock of seagulls darted gracefully toward the Gulf, above all the mayhem. I felt like the seagulls, gliding effortlessly along, pushed by the free air without a care in the world. I mean, what was there to worry about?

Drug Lords and *Federales*

To my amazement, we finished all the paperwork at the border in less than an hour. That is, we finished after I ponied up 550 bucks with the promise from the Mexican Government that I'd get $400 of it back upon safe return. Had the IRS possibly infiltrated Mexico? I stuck the car permit on the front windshield and pulled out of the secure customs compound.

Our only hitch at the crossing had been the Federal Police's inspection of the car's trunk. The bundles of electrical wire perplexed the soldier. Was I up to some mischief? I quickly explained that the car was electric. "*No petro,*" I said. "*Loco gringos.*"

The soldier never modified his tough face, but shut the trunk and motioned us on. We didn't need any more major problems this morning. Only twenty minutes earlier we had avoided a small mishap. Tesla's Model S does not come equipped with a spare, jack, or lug wrench. With some effort, I had bought a spare, specially made in Indiana and shipped to me in Louisiana, and got my hands on a jack and matching lug wrench. All had been loaded in the car, or so I thought, but as we approached the border, the jack was nowhere to be found.

Pondering whether we should turn around and go back to the Walmart in McAllen, like a magician performing a trick, Steve found a small scissor jack in the bed of his truck. This was incredibly fortuitous. With the Tesla's limited clearance, this was the only type of jack that would work. What a mess if we had a flat on some desolate road only to discover we had no jack.

Ten minutes later we were on the busy streets of Reynosa. The industrial border city of half a million was once a hot spot for vice and partying, a place where American college boys went for the anything-goes atmosphere or to lose their virginity. Sadly, it's now one of the most dangerous cities in the world, an epicenter of the Mexican drug war, known for endless running gun battles, dismemberments, and bodies hanging from overpasses. Fortunately, tourists are not typically on the target list.

I weaved around numerous potholes on the lookout for drug lords. I wasn't sure what a drug lord looked like, but almost anything seemed plausible. The four-lane road resembled any American street through a run-down neighborhood, but the cars were older, more worn out, and the drivers crisscrossed the pavement without regard for traffic-control measures.

I'm quite familiar with Mexico, having lived here for a year about a decade ago when working in the oil industry. The northern border region is one of the few areas of the country where I truly feel uncomfortable, so I'd hoped we'd be able to shoot over to our first destination, Saltillo, non-stop. We could quickly cover the two hundred miles in a few hours and put the worst of the border area behind us.

Constantly checking the road signs, mirrors, and GPS, I sliced in and out of the hectic traffic. Where would a wrong turn here lead? The sights were minimal, mostly pedestrians and businesses.

• • •

Only a month earlier, on a Saturday afternoon, journalist Michael Deibert made a turn down a side street here and found himself eye to eye with the unthinkable—a cartel roadblock manned by machine gun-toting enforcers inspecting every car. Fortunately for Michael, the gunmen were apparently looking for someone other than him.

About two months after we passed through here, the city erupted with firefights and roadblocks. Over a two-month period, sixty-four ambush killings, or *ejecuciones,* took place on these streets. Let's get the hell out of here as fast as possible, before we run into a drug lord who wants to reduce his fossil fuel emissions!

• • •

Five more minutes and we found ourselves outside of town. We passed something completely useless to us, a nice, American-style PEMEX Station. In another fifteen minutes, we found ourselves on HWY 40 without a hitch.

I let out a big sigh. We were finally on our way, not simply physically, but also mentally. Even the night before, I had lingering doubts. Would we actually go through with this? Would Dean or I have second thoughts at the moment of truth?

One of the biggest impediments to the trip had been actually finding someone to go with me. Plenty of people said, "Hell, yeah." But of the dozens, only Dean climbed in the truck the day before. Some probably had second thoughts after thinking it over, but most suffered from the fear that if they missed a crucial meeting, deadline, or special social event, fire, brimstone, and eternal damnation would arrive on their doorsteps.

Dean synced up his electronic tablet and put on some Jimmy Buffet, "Wonder Why We Ever Go Home," and I set the cruise control on 50 mph, a speed that should give us about 325 miles of range under optimum conditions.

The scenery seemed to be turning a little more tropical, the land a little more hilly. Or was it? Was my mind hoping for and expecting a change? The terrain rushing by induced trepidation. I was no stranger to traveling. Through work, recreation, or my hiking and climbing when younger, I'd been to over thirty countries, much of it far from tourist circuits, off the beaten track. But I had never undertaken anything like this. Few had.

For this trip, we had no corporate or government sponsorship or aid. We had no logistical support, or anyone to scout the way. We had only our wits. This wasn't some adventure or reality TV show manufactured by Hollywood, where hidden off-camera lay the safety of a support crew and corporate resources. We had somewhere to go, to prove that something could be done, to satisfy our own wants, egos, and needs, and we had finite assets. Every fiber of our bodies and souls would try to make it happen, if it could be done.

Before the trip, I had reached out to several people for help. One was Mike Nelson, a McAllen native and writer of travel books catering to people driving south of the border. Mike travels frequently to Mexico, and is constantly updating his webpage with current information. The other source was Sanborn's, an all-service travel company with offices scattered along the Mexican/American border, that provides an array of services to travelers heading south. That was it.

Twenty minutes outside of town my cell phone rang. It was Steve.

I answered, "What's up?"

"You make it?"

"Yeah, we're out of town and on the road."

"Just checking. The Texas cops stopped us after we dropped you off. They saw us headed to the border with the car, and then on the way back without the car. They wanted to know what's up. We told them the story. They told us you wouldn't make it two hours until somebody steals that fancy car."

"We'll take it under advisement," I said. "They've gotta catch us first. Gotta go."

I relayed the comforting news to Dean and looked at my door mirror. Prior to our departure, we had spray-painted two of the Tesla's fenders with temporary paint, one red and one gray, trying to mimic bondo in hopes this might cheapen the value of the car in the eyes of any potential robbers.

As I inspected our artwork, I slowed for a military checkpoint at the state line between Tamaulipas and Nuevo León. The *policía* checked our papers and asked a few questions. As they did, one of the officers rubbed on the paint and it easily transferred itself to his hands. He looked to his partner. My shaky Spanish and an interpolation of their faces told me they wondered what we were hiding.

"*Arte*," I said, spitting out the Spanish translation of "art," the only Spanish word I could conjure up. Is there a word for "fake bondo?"

A few anxious seconds passed. The two policemen scrutinized the car suspiciously, but a honking horn turned their attention to a car behind us. "Okay," one of them finally said and handed me my paperwork.

Steve's call and the serious nature of the checkpoint reminded me we were not on an Americanized vacation, a week sunning in Cancún or fishing in Costa Rica. It saddled me with a strange sensation of both rapture and foreboding.

I pulled forward twenty or thirty feet to let Dean drive. I'd take over the navigation. Less than an hour later I realized what a mistake this had been. As the day passed, Dean developed the annoying habit of playing with his tablet, and worse, video recording the trip from behind the steering wheel. In Mexico, strict, even rigid defensive driving while manning the steering wheel is best for long life expectancy. The driver and director had become one. I'd be up early enough every morning to claim the driver's seat, at least until the new surroundings had worn off for Dean.

Now on the open road, the landscape unfolded through my six-dollar, truck-stop sunshades, an isolated stretch of rolling sage. Snow-capped mountains loomed ahead, but along the modern freeway, the land lay almost devoid of human presence.

•   •   •

Few, if any, border crossings in the world constitute such an abrupt transformation as the Rio Grande. Paris is a drastic change from Baghdad, but if you drive the roughly two thousand miles along the route, the changes in culture and people are gradual.

Crossing from Texas to Mexico is stark—first world to poverty, order to disorder, lawful to a place where the military and Federal Police wear masks to hide their identity.

We passed an isolated PEMEX station, where Dean wanted to stop and get a Coke and some peanuts. I protested, at least long enough to forestall this as we passed the crossover.

Though traveling through much of Mexico is generally safe, this stretch of land and HWY 40 in particular are somewhat notorious. The two hundred-square-mile wedge of earth bound by Monterrey, Nuevo Laredo, and Reynosa is often called the triangle of death. And HWY 40 is the site of the 2012 Cadereyta Jiménez massacre, in which the drug cartels decapitated and mutilated forty-nine people and left them on the side of the road. Hopefully, the nonstop ride would put us out of this area by noon. This was hardly the place to stop and loiter in an expensive, new car.

Sure enough, we passed a heavily armed patrol of Federal Police, two modern, heavy-duty Ford trucks painted a slick black and white. The soldiers, clad in body armor, stood in the backs of the trucks, their machine guns handy, eyeing every car with unsmiling, alert eyes. Only an hour across the border, the reminders of the ugly side of this land lay everywhere.

The rest of the morning passed eventless other than my constant checking of the Tesla's range meter. For most of the morning, it suggested that we would only get the EPA-rated range of 265 miles per full charge. This was considerably lower than I'd expected, because in Louisiana I'd averaged well over 300 miles a charge at this speed.

Was it the load? We'd packed light in hopes of increasing our range and nimbleness, a bag each with four changes of clothes, two sleeping bags, laptop computers, a phone, shaving kit, portable commode, and a tent. Additionally, we had a bag with electrical and mechanical tools and extension cords, a cardboard box with a few maps and three guidebooks, and of course, a half-dozen rolls of Charmin toilet paper and box of maximum-strength Imodium. Total cargo: six hundred to seven hundred pounds. We'd forage for everything else.

By noon, we skirted around the north side of Monterrey, Mexico's third largest and wealthiest city, the evidence of the more than three million residents visible in the thick cloud of smog hovering over the city and seen easily from a distance. Rising above the pollution, jagged, green mountains encased the metropolis.

Leaving Monterrey, we climbed up a high, barren mountain pass to Saltillo. Steep, gray rock rubble slopes tumbled down steeply to the road, only occasionally broken by scant yucca. I had read Sam Chamberlain's account of his time in Saltillo and Monterrey during the Mexican-American War. Filled with amusing stories of American soldiers wandering the colonial streets and flooding the area's cantinas and fiestas, he also told the harrowing story of his own trip through this pass. Called the Pass of Death by the cavalrymen, the narrow passage was a favorite haunt of highwaymen and vultures, both leaving the pass pockmarked with cadavers and bleached-whited bones. After the war, Sam moved on to scalp hunting, his story the inspiration for Cormac McCarthy's modern classic, *Blood Meridian*.

My fears grew—not of bandits but of the range meter, now showing that we would get only 80 percent of the rated miles. Would we even make it to Saltillo? The destination and range now almost matched.

As we crested the pass, the projected range increased 15 to 20 percent. We'd make it to Saltillo, but with less safety factor than I'd hoped.

Around 1:30 p.m., we rolled under the large *Bienvenidos a Saltillo* sign spanning the road. We looked for a hotel capable of housing us with Western comforts and, more importantly, a handy 240-volt socket where we could charge the car.

I'd gotten a tip: the Hotel Emperial and Trailer Park. We punched it into the GPS and, to my amazement, it popped up on the little screen—straight ahead, a half mile on the right. Thank God for modern technology. What in the hell did Columbus do?

Pulling in, I saw window air conditioners protruding from the rooms that were likely powered by 240-volt outlets. Unfortunately, none of the hotel's clerks spoke English, but with my Spanglish, I got the hotel clerk to show me one of the rooms. I quickly checked the AC socket, a standard NEMA 6-20. I had an adapter for the plug.

"*Bueno*," I said. "*Cuenta questa?*"

"*770 pesos*," the clerk said.

"Internet?"

The young man nodded.

About fifty-five dollars. In New York or DC I have paid five times as much, no internet included, but with a rat thrown in free. "I'll take it," I said.

With the aid of a 200-foot, 50-amp extension cord, I rigged up a connection that worked. The Tesla was charging at 18 amps. It would be fully charged by nine the next morning. I sat down and analyzed the day's trip. We'd gone 196 miles with 41 miles left in the batteries. Not bad considering our heavy load and the fact we'd climbed from sea level to Saltillo, elevation 5,200 feet.

Not having eaten all day and still in two-day-old clothes, I left Dean with the car and walked down the town's main street to a small convenience store.

Saltillo, the oldest town in northeast Mexico, founded in 1577, sits on an arid plain at the north end of the Chihuahua Desert on the other side of a mountain pass from its much larger neighbor, Monterrey. Though the city has over 700,000 residents, like most Mexican towns, it's much smaller, geographically, than American cities of equal population, probably equating in size and services to an American town with 150,000 people. Despite its nice plaza and colonial buildings, most of the town had square, stucco buildings, mostly white, tan, or pink. The architecture, the towering mountains surrounding the city, and the clean, dry air produced the ambiance of a frontier settlement. In the last two hundred years, the old Spanish city had been conquered by the American Army and Pancho Villa.

We were finally on our way. We were here. We had crossed the states of Tamaulipas and Nuevo León, and into Coahuila. Under a stunning blue sky, I felt the isolation of a foreign land, but also an unleashed surge of autonomy and the draw of the open road. Satisfaction oozed over my soul. One day complete. No small accomplishment, but every day would doubtfully be this easy.

I stepped into the store, picked up four bottles of water, two sandwiches, and some snacks. With relief still filling me, I put the goods on the counter. "*Buenos tardes,*" I said to the short, sun-beaten, elderly man behind the counter as I looked up at a poster on the wall, a bronze beauty in a skimpy bikini touting a brand of Mexican beer. Pulling some money from my wallet, I nodded to the poster. "*Dónde este ella?*"

"*Estados Unidos,*" the man said casually as he bagged the goods.

"Too bad," I said, picking up the bags, "I'm going the other way."

Don't Come

The next morning I had a chilly shower as the hotel had no heater. The sexy Mexican weather gal said it was ten degrees Celsius. I'm an engineer, but have no clue what that is. Somewhere in the forties, I guessed. With our batteries fully charged, we were on the road by nine-fifteen, me behind the wheel. Dean could film all he wanted today.

• • •

The previous evening had not been completely without drama. Walking Saltillo's main street late in the day, Dean had stumbled onto a raid by the *Federales*, locked and loaded, on some establishment right around the corner from the hotel.

While I looked over some maps for the next day's trip, scanned my emails, and tried to get some writing done, Dean spent a few hours googling Saltillo only to determine it was a hotbed of the drug trade and the Mexican government's current war on the cartels. Just in the last year, bodies had been found, hacked and deposited along the city's streets.

I did a quick check of the US State Department's travel warnings for Mexico. Though the warnings are often

overblown, this is what our government has to say about
Coahuila:

> Defer non-essential travel to the State of Coahuila. The
> State of Coahuila continues to experience high rates of
> violent crimes and narcotics-related murders. Trans-
> national criminal organizations continue to compete
> for territory and coveted border crossings to the United
> States. Violent crime, including murder, kidnapping,
> and armed carjacking, continues to be a major concern
> in the cities. . . .

If there was any good news, the American researchers had less to
say about Coahuila than the three other states we'd cross in the first
few days. More concerning were the general statements. "Carjacking and highway robbery are serious problems in many parts of the
border region. . . . There are indications that criminals target newer
and larger vehicles, especially dark-colored SUVs. However, even
drivers of old sedans and buses coming from the United States have
been targeted. . . ."

A brand new Tesla, non-negotiable price $79,900, with Loui-
siana plates, would certainly be a prime target.

Dean, being the Army-intel type, made me get up off the bed
and rewire the extension cord charging the car so he could better
secure the hotel room. Then, just after dark and against my advice,
he took off on a solo stroll around the neighborhood to see if he
could find anything else interesting.

He must have found something, and when he returned Ol'
Montezuma got his revenge. Dean spent most of the night either
puking or with his lesser half secured to the commode.

Ever leery, I was up early that morning, repeatedly infusing myself with nicotine in hopes I might get any mishaps out of the way before we hit the road.

Dean pulled the portable commode from the trunk and put it in a handier place, the back seat, while I checked my voicemail. I had a few delightful messages from friends, ranging from well-wishes to inquiries about what I was smoking. On Facebook, Dean had posted one of the videos he'd made the day before while he was supposed to be driving, and it now circled through cyberspace. How did mankind survive before cellphones and iPads?

Today's drive was only 160 miles to Matehuala, at about the same elevation of 5,200 feet, but would require traversing an 8,000-foot pass on the climb out of Saltillo. We got caught up in a six-lane traffic mess that cost us fifteen minutes, and my cell phone rang three times. I didn't answer it. Didn't everybody know I was off the grid? Ideally, I would love to have thrown the damn thing in the Rio Grande the day before, but it might come in handy, especially if we got in a pinch. We were twenty-first-century Balboas, not the real thing!

Stuck in traffic, I did text my sister. She had sent me a nasty text the night before, chastising me for just slipping out of town without saying goodbye. Back in Louisiana, the family was supposed to be getting together this week for my brother's birthday.

I had kept most of the family out of the loop about the trip, mostly because I didn't want to hear the lectures about safety.

My family is a typical American bunch, that is, typically dysfunctional. I love them all dearly, but I could have long ago gotten rich and famous writing a book about them, or better yet, creating a reality TV show. Louisiana seems to be all the rage on the reality TV scene today, but all the eccentrics don't live in swamps or hunt ducks. I guess there's a chance (though slim) that I'm the screwball and they're normal.

Hoping to have appeased my sister with a short text, we hit the open road, climbing up the rugged pass. It felt good to put Saltillo behind us. With the morning, I felt a sense of rebirth. Back in the States, across the fruited plain, people were settling in for their daily routine. Not us. We dared to go forward into uncertainty.

In less than a half hour, we found ourselves sputtering along over rolling terrain with a few snowcapped mountains off to our east. The colors gave way to dry chaparral as we entered the cool, open plains of the Chihuahua Desert, populated with thick, tall cacti.

This area was even more devoid of humans than the previous day's trip. The Mexicans call it *La Frontera*, and no wonder. It's a playground for the drug cartels.

If you read some of the statistics about the countries we'd be crossing, and this region of Mexico especially, you might think we were morons. It's true that the official murder, kidnapping, carjacking, and robbery rates in many of these countries are some of the highest in the world. And more than eighty thousand people have been killed in the Mexican drug war since 2006, not to mention another twenty-five thousand or so classified as "missing." Worse, the cops are as likely to be part of the local underworld as not.

The stats can be a little misleading for foreigners. Most of the crimes are criminal-on-criminal violence, or include other parties with a vested interest—police, journalists, wealthy citizens, politicians—involved in one way or another with political infighting, drug wars, and the like.

All things being equal, the drug cartels would prefer to avoid the tourists. Most tourists (not those masquerading as tourists) that get killed simply get caught in the crossfire of the turf war, are mistaken for somebody else, or are moseying around somewhere they shouldn't be.

The robbery, carjacking, and kidnapping, on the other hand, is much worse than in the States, as the statistics indicate. Mexico is the worst country in the world for kidnappings, and those victims are more likely to be people outside the drug trade.

I don't have any official data, but based on my experience working and traveling in these countries, often driving, crime in Central America occurs much differently from the States. In New Orleans, even in the tourist areas of the French Quarter or the Warehouse district, it can be very dangerous after dark, especially if you're going to one of the finer restaurants hidden away on a side street. On the other hand, you can drive the ninety miles between Baton Rouge and New Orleans through the rural and somewhat poor river parishes on a two-lane road, even late at night, and it's very safe.

The opposite holds true in Latin America. In the cities, especially around the businesses and tourist areas, there's less chance for malice. The security presence is high. As long as you don't wander off aimlessly, and get in at a reasonable hour, you're likely to be fine. It's in the no-man's-land between the cities where problems lurk. There's typically no cell service and little police presence.

I've noticed something over the years—a common scenario by which tourists get into trouble. This situation involves foreigners in a nice car going to a little or midsized city and staying a few days, driving around, being visible. If you're white or black down here, you get noticed. You're different, probably taller and dressed differently from everybody else. They know you're a stranger. When you do this, the bad guys take notice. You have to leave sometime, and when you head out into the sticks, they pounce.

Anybody that really knows anything about the Latin drug trade knows that the biggest sin is encroaching on someone else's territory. They shoot first and ask questions later. If they got the wrong person, at least they sent the message. White guys milling around an out-of-the-way town for a few days in a Tesla—well, you figure it out.

This may seem over-the-top, but in *El Sicario, The Autobiography of a Mexican Assassin,* the anonymous hit man who undertook hundreds of kidnappings and murders in his career, mostly in northern Mexico, bluntly stated that his daily routine entailed: "Patrol the city. Look out for new people in town, new vehicles."

Much of Mexico and Central America off the tourist circuit is truly a wild west, especially if you don't have any security or look wealthy. Over the years, I've developed a plan. Really, it's only common sense. Drive the main roads during the day. Drive point to point, no stopping or loitering. Arrive in a town, park the car in a secure location for the night, and generally keep a low profile. Then get up and be on the road as early as you can. I'm guessing thugs and drug dealers like to sleep in. Don't get caught in the boondocks with dark approaching. Know where the bad areas are and try to avoid them. Adhere to these rules strictly, especially the notion of constant movement. If you see something that worries you, find a safe place, contact the authorities, and wait.

These measures are more problematic in an electric car, but employing them as best you can reduces risk, in my mind anyway, to acceptable levels. Lastly, these endeavors are not for penny-pinchers. Nothing you bring with you, even a car, is worth getting into a scrap in a foreign land. Factories around the world are rolling out computers and cars by the thousands every day. I promise you, you can get another one. Come to grips with this before you depart.

• • •

During the day, we only passed five or six ramshackle little villages. The tin roofs sat on wood or cinder-block structures between dirt roads. The only tourist attraction in the area was the Buena Vista Battlefield, about twenty miles off the road, where General Zachary Taylor and five thousand Americans defeated Santa Anna and sixteen thousand of his men during the Mexican-American War. I would love to have seen it, as the battle constituted a significant portion of my second novel. But this was not a sightseeing trip. We had road to cover, and later in the day, we'd be glad we hadn't made any side trips.

The good news was the Tesla's range had increased significantly, easing my worries of the previous day. Our range meter indicated that at our current driving rate, we'd get 330 miles on a single charge. Wow! Maybe the batteries hadn't been fully charged the day before, or maybe it was thin air at a mile above sea level. I didn't care.

The sparse, open road was uncomfortably lonely, with only a few vehicles coming and going. To my surprise, during the day we were only forced to go through one *Federale* stop. The southbound road had only a four-car wait, but the northbound queue stretched more than a mile, mostly 18-wheelers. The *policía* were obviously worried about northbound cargo much more than southbound.

The car's graffiti again aroused the guards' suspicion, but after a few questions and some explaining, the courteous policeman inquired in English, "Is your wife mad at you?"

"*No esposa*," I said and everybody, including the tough-looking policemen, laughed as they waved us on. I turned to Dean. "Tonight, we're going to rub that stupid paint off."

The rest of the day went smoothly, my only concern the hordes of sheep and occasional horses grazing in the federal highway's right-of-way. If we hit one of those, that might be only slightly better than an encounter with the local bandits. The best-case scenario would be a busted window, and I'm sure getting a Tesla window in Mexico would be fairly impossible. It has no North American operations outside of Canada and the United States.

By 1:00 p.m., we came through a small pass and coasted into the dusty, desert town of Matehuala, population about seventy thousand. Local legend says the name is derived from an indigenous phrase that means "Don't come."

Latin Electricity

After a few wrong turns we pulled into the hotel and RV park: Las Palmas Halfway Inn—halfway across the desert.

The rooms had window ACs with 240-volt sockets, right where we could drive up and plug in without even using the extension cord. I inspected the sockets, standard NEMA 6-20s, just like we'd used the night before. I checked the outlet with my voltmeter, 240 volts. Good. Thrilled, we purchased two rooms, one hundred dollars American.

Then I tried to plug in the car. Tesla's charging adapter would not produce the little green light that showed it was charging. I quickly tried the AC in Dean's room. Same result. I then pulled out a standard 120-volt extension cord that might be used for a set of hedge clippers in the States. Same result. Tesla's adapter checks for several things—ground, circuit, thermal faults, etc. And if these don't check out, it will not allow a charge.

• • •

Charging a Tesla can be an art as much as a science. Though I'm very technically oriented, electricity was a subject I struggled to understand all my life. My only formal education in the field, the college-level course in circuits required for all engineers to graduate, produced a D on my transcript—and I'd been lucky and quite happy to receive the minimal passing score in the science that confounded me.

In recent months I'd undertaken a newfound interest in the subject and spent hours trying to understand the basic concepts: 240-volt electricity, or what comes from the big sockets we plug our dryers or air conditioners into, can supply the most energy, but equally important for charging, much larger amperages can be supplied with 240-volt power.

Amperes, or amps, represent the rate that the electricity is available, and hence, larger available amps means faster charging. For example, 240 volts at 20 amps can fully charge the Tesla in eighteen hours. Two hundred and forty volts at 40 amps can charge it in nine hours. With 120-volt power, or the simple two-pronged plug we have in our houses for lamps, etc., the charging time increases by a factor of four or more. It will take standard 120-volt, 12-amp power almost three days to fully charge the Tesla. We needed 240-volt power to have any success.

Before the trip, I'd rigged up about twenty different adapters for 240-volt power, a range of three- and four-prong plugs used in this hemisphere. There are actually more than fifty different 240-volt plugs in use, but I thought I had most of the frequently-used plugs. The good news is that, while in Mexico and Central America, the available electric grid, at least in theory, mimics that in the United States, supplying consumers with standard 120- or 240-volt, 60-Hertz frequency power, through a variety of NEMA (National Electrical Manufacturers Association) sockets.

• • •

Now I had the right plug and voltage, but something wasn't right with the power supply. I looked around at the hotel's wiring, a hodgepodge of electrical lines, hastily patched into rooms. Some of the ACs were wired directly without a plug. Who knew what was really inside the walls, and what this mangle of electrical patchwork at the hotel could handle. A seasoned electrical engineer would be lying if he thought he knew.

To put it mildly, in Latin America, electrical codes and standards aren't as uniform or rigid as in the States. There is a never-ending array of sockets, and though these may be designed for certain voltages and amperes, they are, let's say, adapted for many different uses.

I met with the hotel maintenance man, asking him if he had some portion of the hotel that was new. All my questions brought negative responses, so Dean and I did a little checking. The town had one other major hotel, The Casa Real. It was next door. We drove over right away. The hotel had window AC units.

Inside, I was greeted by an attractive Mexican gal fit for the front desk of the Mondrian in West Hollywood. What the hell is a woman like this doing in the middle of the desert? I had recently read an article in some paper that the drug lords had a fondness for Mexican beauty queens, and vice versa.

I spoke up in my best Spanish. "Good afternoon. We've got an electric car we need to charge. Can I see if I can charge it here? Can I test it on one of your rooms?"

My charm worked. She smiled and called the hotel's maintenance chief, a short, friendly man. He let us in a room. The window AC units were only 120 volts, and the Tesla's adapter wouldn't produce a green clearance light while plugged in.

I asked the man if he had a 240-volt socket anywhere I could use. He promptly led me to the hotel's laundry room and pointed to a rough socket on the wall. I didn't know if I had the adapter, but more disconcerting was the Christmas tree of wires leading to it.

I studied the setting and the hotel's wiring. It was doubtful the shoddy wiring could damage the Tesla as the charging adapter will not let it access power if something's not right. Could this makeshift setup damage the adapter?

The bigger problem was what the car could do to the socket. The Tesla allows the charging rate or amperage to be set before charging. In the States, if the socket is rated for 20 amps, you'd likely set the charging rate at 18 amps to be a little safe, as I did the previous evening. If you overpower the socket, the fuse just trips. Then, you simply reset the fuse and lower the charging rate. If the system is not properly wired or doesn't have the correct breaker fuse, who knows what can happen? I didn't fancy sitting in a Mexican prison for burning down a hotel.

Dean and I got back in the car and rode around town for about an hour looking for somewhere to charge. We found four or five hotels, scruffy ten-dollar-a-night types. We traversed the compact city center, a traffic nightmare, getting nothing but a glance at Matehuala's huge but unfinished cathedral. Construction began on the mammoth stone structure in 1906. Things happen slowly here.

We finally stopped at an automotive shop where nobody spoke English. Fifteen minutes later the manager was more confused than we were. Like most of the people in the crowded city *centro* who stared at us with immense, prying eyes, he surely wondered who these silly gringos were, driving around town in a fancy sports car looking for electricity.

Desperation setting in, and out of options, we returned to the Las Palmas wondering when or if we'd get to leave Matehuala. We had motored around enough. The little desert town looks small and simple on first inspection, but just over a year earlier, it had made international news. The mayor-elect and his aid had been gunned down here by one of the drug cartels as they left a birthday party.

We rode to the back of the hotel where RVs were allowed to park. There, they had five or six old 120-volt sockets. We plugged the Tesla's adapter into one of the sockets and finally got it to charge at 12 amps—not much, but enough to add about 60 miles of range to the car overnight. I quickly calculated that with the power we had left over from the day's trip, we'd have about 190 miles of range by 7:00 a.m.. San Luis Potosí was 133 miles to the south.

We were charging, though minimally. I didn't really feel like staying in underwhelming Matehuala another night. We'd go to San Luis Potosí the next morning and try to find a better source of current. At least we'd be out of the desert and into the more densely populated areas.

I looked at the late-day sun and sighed as I started to realize how difficult this might be. Had the first day been the exception? It would likely take all of our creative juices and ad-libbing to keep the sleek, high-tech machine moving south every day.

Inspecting the hotel, I eerily noticed we were one of only three or four guests, and the only foreigners. The night before, I had done some internet research on the Las Palmas Inn, finding a trove of pictures with dozens of American RVs lined up at the once-popular stop. Obviously, those days were gone. As I had witnessed on the road earlier in the day, almost nobody, Mexican or American, traversed this route anymore. Vacationers pouring south to enjoy Mexico's treasures and treats were other victims of the drug war. I plucked an orange off a tree on the hotel's lawn, peeled it, and began to eat. Now *this* was foraging.

Out of the Desert and Into the Tropics

I was up early the next morning. My alarm clock: Matehuala's roosters. I took a shower and plucked two disgusting gray hairs from my bangs. So far, the digestive tract had been fine, but the previous evening I had eaten my first prepared food on the trip, some fried cheese sticks from the hotel restaurant. I felt fine, but I was no rookie to Mexico, and my stomach was likely more delicate than Dean's. When south of the border, I never stop wondering before I put anything in my mouth: Will this give me the runs?

Since the hotel had Wi-Fi, I briefly passed over my email. The world had not stopped rotating without me. Somehow, my email account had been tagged in the computer universe, and my daily list of spam included a rather risqué email from *Playboy*, complete with full-body portraits of hot, unclad women. Of course, I delete this trash every day, but as with all spam, it's appropriate protocol to open it first and briefly scan the contents before deleting, just to make sure it is indeed spam, and not something important I need to address. Attention to detail is a key to success in any occupation.

Dean walked into my room, dressed and ready for a 7:00 a.m. departure. He looked no worse for the wear, back on his feet from the mild bout of stomach tumbling.

I stepped out and inspected the car, shaking my head. "I thought you were going to scrub that fake paint off the car last night? What'd you do, take a nap instead?"

"*Me?* . . . You told me you'd do the washing. After you screwed up the charging yesterday, I guess you decided to muddle up the washing too. I sure hope you weren't up all night finding another country paradise like this for us to enjoy tomorrow night."

"Whatever. We ain't got time to worry with it now. Let's get on the road."

In no time, we happily said goodbye to Matehuala, hopefully never to return. If they have rednecks in Mexico, this would likely be an ideal gathering spot.

Under overcast skies and with Dean behind the wheel, we yearned for straight, flat tarmac. The hasty charging the previous evening didn't go as well as I'd thought, but we had 169 miles of range to go the 133 miles to San Luis Potosí.

In Mexico, when you leave town, and I mean almost *exactly* at the city line, the cell phone service ends abruptly. Not what you want when headed out across a barren desert hosting a war between the *Federales* and drug cartels with little spare juice in the tank.

The landscape was again scrubby, a few little towns polluted with trash, the people seemingly living hand to mouth, a testament to people's struggle for survival at the most fundamental level. But on the open road, North America's second largest desert appeared to be one of the few places on the continent barely impacted by humans, the scrub, yucca, and Joshua trees stretching beyond the horizon. Just south of Matehuala, we crossed the Tropic of Cancer. We were now officially in the tropics.

We plowed along bravely, surveying the emptiness, the only sight a bad wreck in the middle of the road that probably had no survivors, a '60s Volkswagen Beetle, upside down and mangled. This area of the desert, known as the Bolsón de Mapimí, has long been a no-man's-land and haven for bandits. The huge, barren basin, spanning several hundred miles in all directions, is bounded by mountains and without rivers. Unwanted by the Spanish because of its lack of minerals or arid land, it was once the haunt of Comanches fleeing the Texas Rangers.

• • •

This isolated stretch of road is the site where, in 2011, US Homeland Security agent Jaime Zapata was killed by one of the cartels as he drove south to Mexico City in a suburban. His partner, Víctor Ávila, shot twice in the leg, lived to tell the chilling story.

Out of nowhere, two SUVs raced up behind the Americans, one storming past them. The two SUVs, filled with a dozen machine gun-armed men, fired away and rammed the Americans off the road. Eighty-three spent casings were found at the scene. In the mayhem, the agents tried to explain that they were American agents.

One of the assailants yelled, "*Me vale madre.*" Translation: "I don't give a fuck."

Ávila likely survived because the American suburban was armored. The gun hands, later caught, confessed that they did not know who was in the car. They simply wanted the tricked-out suburban. We didn't have any armor. No wonder I'd become a pack-a-day smoker in just a few days.

• • •

We only suffered through one *Federale* stop where they waved us through without correspondence—the *policía* only worried about the long northbound line. But twenty miles later, a federal policeman pulled us over, lights flashing. Mexican cops swooping in on you, especially on a vacant road and from out of nowhere, is an unsettling experience. A few antsy seconds passed as the officer walked to the car.

With an empty stare, neither hostile nor friendly, the gentleman asked about the paint on the flashy car.

"*Tourista,*" Dean said from behind the wheel, playing dumb. "*Norte Americano*, we go to Veracruz."

The officer turned to me, then the painted fender again. A few seconds passed and he handed Dean his passport and driver's permit. "*Bueno.*"

Dean smiled at me. "I don't speak a lick of Spanish, but playing dumb seems to work better than that combination of broken Spanish mixed with your country-ass accent. That only confuses them."

Late in the morning, as we drove through a light drizzle, the GPS and range meter told us we'd make it into San Luis Potosí with fifty miles to spare. Out of nowhere, the city popped up out of the desert. Here, isolation transitions into a dense urban landscape quickly. As soon as we reached the city line, my cell phone rang. There's no escape, I thought, and didn't answer as I looked for street signs. The night before, I'd done some internet research. Most of the city's western hotels were in the southeast quarter of town.

In no time, we found ourselves tangled in some road construction, north- and southbound lanes creeping along over a single dirt road. Ironically, we got stuck behind a two-wheeled cart pulled by a donkey for almost a mile. What a contrast—the Tesla waiting on the donkey.

Though Dean had refrained from video recording all day as he drove the open, almost vacant road, now as we bumped over construction joints, weaved around dumptrucks, backhoes, and oncoming traffic, he decided it was time to videorecord the donkey!

"Give me that camera," I scoffed, "If you have to film that old mule, let me do it."

Dean moved the camera to his left hand and out of reach. "No, you'll screw it up like the paint washing."

As if he needed some more distractions, Dean spoke to the camera, "Randy hates it when I drive and film."

I pulled out a piece of Nicorette gum, trying to extract it from its little tin container. The wrapper is a disaster, designed like a Pentecostal preacher might fashion a chastity belt for his daughter. If any of the gum rubs against the metal or cellophane package, everything gets mushed together and you can't get the metal out of the gum. After twiddling with the gum over the bumpy road for a few minutes, I threw the entire contraption out the window and grabbed a cigarette. Oh well, it's the thought that counts.

Somehow, we made it through the construction without a mishap and in a few minutes were cruising the Avenida Benito Juárez that housed a couple dozen hotels ranging from upper-end establishments, like the Holiday Inn, to bottom-end shanties not fit for convicts. The area had a Walmart, Pizza Hut, and three nice strip clubs (none of the latter for us—the State Department mentioned they were hangouts for drug lords and carjackers). Mexico and the States do have a few things in common.

Despite three passes, and me going in and looking at four different hotels, we found no place to charge the car in more than an hour of determined searching. Frustration setting in, we pulled into the Hotel Maria Dolores. Tired of beating around the bush, I asked if they would show me all the rooms. Walking the hotel with one of the clerks, I found a room with a window AC unit and an exterior socket, 240 volts. "*Perfecto*," I said.

I purchased the night without even checking the rate. Pulling around to the room, I plugged in the Tesla's charging adapter and got a green light. I set the charge rate to 18 amps and calculated that the car would be fully charged by nine the next morning.

Whoa, I thought, apprehension setting in. This was getting tough. We were in a town of almost a million people, and it had taken hours to find adequate power. Charging was certainly going to require some unabashed improvisation.

I looked at the flashing green lights on the Tesla's adapter again. Getting the car plugged in and charging at an adequate rate five hundred miles south of the border probably feels something akin to a drug addict getting another hit.

The Riddle of Mexico

Having the afternoon available, Dean and I found time for our first recreation of the trip. Including the twelve-hour trip to McAllen, our four days had been taxing. To my disappointment, the days had been long and exhausting as we crossed four Mexican states. The slow driving, the cumbersome time spent finding a charge, planning for the next day, taking care of emails and calls, and trying to write left little time for sleeping, much less sightseeing. The trip had been all-consuming, but with it a splendid break from our world up north and a sense that we were engaged in something meaningful.

After we spent an hour washing the paint off the car, I changed my pants for the first time since we started. We then took a cab to the center of San Luis Potosí. Perched on a high, dry plateau, it is a lovely four hundred-year-old colonial gem founded to exploit the nearby silver and gold mines. For an hour, Dean and I wandered the tight, cobblestone streets packed with Friday evening pedestrians without seeing a single American.

As the sun waned, I drank my first beer of the trip from the second story of a café overlooking the beautiful *Plaza de Armas* and wonderful, towering cathedral. We snacked on some cheese fries, or at least what had arrived at the table after I ordered French fries covered in cheese—more like potato chips with cheese in a bowl. Must be a Southern thing.

As I sipped my beer, below in the plaza several thousand of the city's residents mingled, happily, looking as if they had not a care in the world, as they'd probably done here for hundreds of years.

The scene reminded me of my fondness for this mesmerizing country. One of the joys of the trip would be seeing much of Latin America up close and personal, off the beaten track and away from tourist spots filled with foreigners that give little hint of the people or places hidden away from the five-star hotels. We were on a voyage that can't be booked by a travel agent, something sought by so many but rarely undertaken.

While Mexico shares a continent and border of almost two thousand miles with the United States, few pairs of bordering countries in the world differ more. Our southern neighbor's land, people, climate, customs, and history are more similar to nations on the other side of the planet than anything most Americans experience every day. It's a land as exotic as anywhere in the world.

What's happened in the last decade with the drug cartels and the significantly increased violence can make Mexico's admirers cry. I keep abreast of the drug war, and am something of an amateur expert. I lived in Mexico in the late 1990s, not as a tourist, but as a contractor for PEMEX, the state-owned oil company. I worked closely with the people and many aspects of the government, I know how the place works.

It still amazes me how quickly the security situation here has devolved. Anything you know about the country that's eight or nine years old can be disregarded. Ten or fifteen years ago, I felt much safer in Mexico than the United States. In all but the most impoverished areas, I felt comfortable wandering the streets alone at all hours of the night.

How this peaceful land of joyous fiestas and sun-splashed pla-zas morphed into armed militias, torture chambers, and chopped-off heads is a complicated story. It's even more intriguing when you consider it happened in a stable, democratic country on the doorstep of the world's only superpower, and in a nation that, at least on a world scale, is rich.

It's a lesson in what happens when petty kickbacks, extor-tion, and trading crimes for bribes (paying your taxes as it's known locally) is woven into the government's fabric. When a rotten sys-tem like that is suddenly injected with billions of illegal dollars, things can spin out of control quickly. The cartels' deeds make the crimes of the American mafia, even in its heyday, seem like school-boy fisticuffs, and the American public is still relatively naïve about this.

When seventy innocent people are executed in San Fernando, only eighty-five miles south of Brownsville, it only makes the back pages of the largest US newspapers.

Before the drug lords consummated the mass murder in San Fernando, they raped the women, then passed out weapons and forced the condemned men to fight each to the death in a sadistic death-sport similar to gladiator matches in ancient Rome.

British journalist Ioan Grillo who has lived in Mexico for more than ten years has written what I consider the best account of the last hideous decade, *El Narco*. It's a page-turner. Ioan's research determined the current fee in Mexico to have someone gunned down is a paltry eighty-five dollars!

Most of Mexico seems to be a contradiction. How can parts of the country be so idyllic and charming while just down the road, often in broad daylight, government forces and heavily armed gangs battle in a daily life-and-death struggle?

I'm often spellbound by this country. Like a rose, it shows off its beauty surrounded by thorns. Eighty years ago, Graham Greene wrote:

> Mexico disappoints—a town seems fine in the evening, and then in daylight the corruptions seep through, the road peters out, the muleteer doesn't show up, the great man on acquaintance becomes strangely muted, and when you get to the gigantic ruins you are too tired to see them.

In many ways, this rings true today. In the last few decades, a true middle class has emerged, and much of the nation's extreme poverty has been vanquished. But Mexico still falls far short of its promise. Few places have more natural resources or physical beauty. The country is the tenth-largest producer of oil in the world, just one example of its wealth, but it lacks almost any social safety net. Class mobility remains difficult. Unlike most of the western world, this is a country where wealth secludes itself far from the road.

Though great strides have been made, it is still very difficult for western business practices and companies to flourish here. Centuries of foreign exploitation have resulted in a Mexican constitution that puts much stricter restraints on citizenship and property ownership than most democratic countries. Paranoia from foreigners' past misbehavior still resonates in the Mexican psyche.

Still, I could sit here for hours and watch the streets teeming with chaos and the constant pushing and shoving in a world where few norms restrict human endeavors. Almost anything goes, almost anything can be bought or bartered, and you are generally on your own to fail or succeed.

This country is a riddle. Eye-tearing injustices sit alongside abundant, smiling eyes and warm greetings that surpass anything in the American South. The cities contain architectural treasures and ancient ruins that rival those of Greece, although you often have to travel down dirt roads festooned with garbage to see them. But unlike America, where everything is beginning to look and act alike, Mexico is a land of perpetual discovery. I truly haven't decided if I envy or pity the inhabitants.

Porfirio Díaz, the Mexican president for thirty years at the end of the nineteenth century, summed up the country and its relationship with its neighbor to the north: Poor Mexico—so far from God and so close to the United States.

In front of the church, a Mexican rock band was setting up a giant stage in the plaza. I wish we could have stayed until the wee hours, drinking too much tequila and wallowing in the nightlife, but we needed to get back to the hotel.

The charging situation at the Hotel Maria Dolores hadn't been as good as I'd initially thought, raising my anxiety level. After the first hour of charging at 18 amps, we'd blown the hotel room's 240-volt breaker. I'd found the breaker and reset it, lowering the charging rate to 16 amps. All looked good before our brief respite on the town, but I wanted to get back to the hotel and check on the car. Maybe we'd get a full charge tonight, and get back on the road so we could get to experience more of Mexico's better side on our glorious trip into a world few westerners experience.

Ancient Mexico

That Friday night the Hotel Maria Dolores hosted a party that included hundreds of Mexican toddlers. As I ate breakfast the next morning, the fifty or so cute, curious faces of the kids playing in the café restored my faith in Mexico and its future.

Our tank full of kilowatts, we left by nine o'clock. Today's trip would be our first real taste of the feared mountains as we planned to skirt around the northeast side of Mexico City to the domain of the Toltecs and their ancient ruins. How would these hills affect the Tesla? We'd surely spend the day anxiously watching the range meter and our rearview mirrors for SUVs racing ahead, but it was Saturday. I wouldn't have to spend the evening returning calls and emails!

As we pulled out of San Luis Potosí, the road quickly transitioned from rolling hills to small mountains. The ride was superlative. The climate and vegetation had become completely tropical, and the mountains and vistas kept my attention.

As had become my routine, I'd spent an hour the night before scouting the route with Google Earth, creating a handwritten spreadsheet of the towns we'd pass. I listed their general size and miles from San Luis Potosí: 134 miles to Queretaro, 210 miles to Tula, and 269 miles to the ancient ruins of Teotihuacan.

Teotihuacan had been our goal, flush with western hotels and tourists, but that morning we learned that, due to the poor roads and large crowds flocking to the site, driving a private car to the ruins was illegal on the weekends. With the engineers and computer scientists at Google on our side, we'd plow on.

Tula, with about 70,000 residents and in the heart of the Toltec area, seemed like a reasonable goal, 210 miles up the road. A staging area for tourists heading to the region's archeological sites, it might have the basic infrastructure required by most western tourists, or mindless *Norte Americanos* looking for adventure. If nothing else, Tula *might* be a secure island in the midst of the drug violence.

The morning was overcast, green row crops filling the space between the mountains. As the day wore on, the sun broke and the land became more populated, the poverty less prevalent. The road became a six-lane freeway for a thirty-mile stretch of what looked like prosperous Mexican suburbs and urban sprawl.

On day five of our odyssey I wondered again, am I a fool? Is this too outlandish? Thus far, the trip had gone well. We'd made it over six hundred miles south of the border, and traversed a major natural obstacle, the Chihuahua Desert, but I still felt uneasy. Charging had been difficult. Even the night before, in a major city, it had been in doubt. What lay ahead? Northern and central Mexico would likely be the most developed areas we'd travel through on the entire trip.

Despite this, I felt drunk with elation, the excitement still bizarre. I had longed for something like this all my life. Most people spend their lives trying to fit in, to be normal. I have always had a fear of anonymity. Was I searching for the *Easy Rider* hidden in me, suppressed by the sameness of everything? Big cities hammer this home for me. We're not supposed to follow life's road but rather choose it. This would certainly be something to tell my kids one day (of course, I have to find a wife while I'm still fertile). But life is something to be enjoyed, not endured, and there's no starting over.

I turned to Dean. "I love this shit. I wish I had your freedom."

"What?"

I repeated myself.

Dean just nodded and glanced at me with a smart-ass smirk. "You can't have it both ways. You can't have the gravy of being a fat-cat boss, and the freedom. Don't work that way."

By early afternoon, we pulled into Tula. The impediments had been minimal, though Dean had started to develop another annoying habit: blaring music while the GPS girl gave me directions at complicated, inadequately signed intersections. I'll say this—a good business person could make a fortune selling the Mexicans some traffic-control signs. One little green sign that said "Exit here for HWY 57 East" would do wonders for the tourists rolling in to spend their greenbacks.

Amazingly, we'd had no *Federale* stops during the day, and our only close call had been a mattress in the road, hidden around a sharp curve. The sheep and goats still grazed in the right-of-way, providing me with constant grief and anxiety.

On the outskirts of Tula, the State Police pulled us over. The stop was routine, but they spent twenty or so minutes mumbling in incomprehensible Spanish as they checked our car and drivers' permits.

Finally in Tula, we looked for a place to charge. Things didn't seem promising. The city center was a tight maze of congested roads, and we got stuck in a miniature version of a third-world Los Angeles traffic jam, except the drivers honked more. Stop signs and lane stripes in Mexico are more suggestions than requirements.

I knew well that here a small fender-bender usually results in all parties hunkering down at the local police station to work out the details.

Searching hotels in our GPS, we stumbled on a golf resort. Surely they had 240-volt power. The hotel was nice, three or four stars by American standards, and the manager, Elita, spoke English.

I explained our situation, leading her and three more of the hotel staff outside to show them the car. I opened the hood, the compartment below it filled only with two sleeping bags and a long extension cord. "*No motor, solamente electrico.*" I opened the trunk to show them I wasn't hiding anything, lifting up the car's charging adapter and pointing to the socket on the side of the car.

The staff's eyes enlarged from elliptical to round, as they oohed, aahed, and mumbled among themselves as they studied the car, carefully inspecting the dashboard and the area under the hood.

I clapped my hands together and pointed south. "*Estados Unidos a Panama, no gasolina.*"

The staff looked at us with both fascination and amusement.

Elita squinted her big brown eyes in a cute gesture, the corners of her lips pointing down. "Yes, is it possible?"

"Maybe," I continued in two languages. "*Necesito 240 voltios.*"

"Okay," Elita said. "We will try."

We spent the next twenty minutes with the hotel's maintenance man walking the hotel and golf course. I couldn't believe it. The golf course had no 240-volt power and all the hotel's air conditioning was directly wired. I did find a 120-volt socket next to the tennis court with a 30-amp fuse beside it. That would at least give us reliable 12-amp charging at 120 volts. We could get sixty miles in sixteen hours.

Elita and the staff were so friendly and helpful, we decided to stay. She let me pull the car onto the golf course to plug up without an extension cord.

"We'll take it," I said to Elita. "Can we catch a cab into town to see the ruins and the church?"

"Of course," she said with a big smile.

As I got the car charging, Dean went up to the room.

Ten minutes later when I got there, I found him laid up in the big nice bed, watching CNN on the first American television station we'd seen in Mexico. The room was plush, with a desk, fridge, and two leather lounge chairs.

Dean found the Louisiana Tech basketball game on some webpage he often used in China, and we got to watch Tech thrash Marshall on national TV. The four-star accommodations were a welcome change of pace.

"They've got some fast internet here," Dean said, leaning back on the big bed. "Let's just stay two or three days and let the car charge on 120 power!"

He was kidding, right? I said, "Don't get too used to this. We're on the road at 8:00 a.m. tomorrow!"

Second Thoughts

We departed the ancient, Toltec city of Tula early on Sunday morning, the church bells banging away. I weaved through the clean, tight streets, bisecting the markets and plazas, abuzz the night before, now lifeless. The Mesoamerican ruins—ancient pyramids and fifteen-foot-high stone warrior statues—guarded the city. Nestled at 6,800 feet, this was Mexico's largest city a thousand years ago.

The natives call these antique towns *pueblos magicos*, magical villages, and I felt it, harmony for my soul, something unique and far from inside-the-beltway America, with its endless monoliths of steel, glass, and concrete.

The city's only scar was the huge PEMEX refinery on the edge of town, the large and abundant smoke stacks blotting the view of the wonderful ruins from a distance.

More than a dozen aggravating speed bumps slowed our pace out of town. These annoying impediments, called *topes* by the Mexicans, cover the roads in urban areas. You'd think they'd at least put up a sign. The *topes* are by no means uniform, and occasionally we'd roll over one that scraped the bottom of the Tesla even at 2 mph. I cringed because the car's batteries line the bottom of the car.

Always leery of eating anything significant before hitting the road, I had a light breakfast of peanuts and *agua* as I drove onto the *autopista*. The drive to Puebla was the best of the trip—the road was smooth, we were waved through the only *Federale* stop along the route, and crossed a 9,000-foot pass. The terrain was similar to West Texas, hilly scrub, but most of the latter half of the drive was dominated by the towering 17,802-foot Popocatépetl Volcano, looming off to our right and belching steam. We passed within twenty miles of the summit.

We left the state of Hidalgo, passed through Tlaxcala into the State of Puebla, and late in the morning rolled into the prehistoric town of Cholula. Bumping over the *topes*, we drove around the town's more than three hundred churches, most probably older than the United States, and the Piramide Tepanapa, a 180-foot Toltec earth pyramid now topped with a yellow-domed church.

The day was cool, the air fresh as we passed through the central square, the streets lined with pink, yellow, and blue hotels and restaurants, all with open-air cafés spilling onto the sidewalks. Classic Mexico. I noticed the young people, pretty girls strolling everywhere, and the cafés filled with more seasoned citizens. I half-expected to see Anthony Quinn sitting at one of the tables, smoking a cigarette and watching the girls.

We inventoried two hotels—no power or ACs. The owner of a third hotel apparently got the bulk of his business by housing the roaming Federal Police as five armored vehicles, guarded by a dozen locked and loaded soldiers, were parked at the hotel. What the *hell* were we doing here?

The owner spoke English and tried to help, but the hotel just didn't have a 240-volt socket.

Moving on to Puebla, we passed the huge 750-acre Volkswagen plant, the biggest automotive plant in North America, employing fifteen thousand people. The plant produced most of the Beetles that roamed the American highways in the '60s and '70s. We checked the Holiday Inn for a charge. No luck.

Dean entered the flashy, new, twenty-story Fiesta Inn, cased in steel and glass, and tried to explain our situation to the clerk. Despite his terrible Spanish, she seemed sympathetic and called the hotel's maintenance man, Hector, who spoke very good English, and told us he had only one 240-volt socket in the hotel kitchen. The manager said we could possibly use it after the kitchen closed at midnight. We could simply pull the car up to the first-floor café and run our extension cord through the restaurant.

"Really?" I said in amazement, but the joy was soon quashed when I inspected the socket—a very rare, four-prong, locking NEMA that I knew we didn't have.

The Tesla now down to a range of about thirty miles, we had one more lead, the Puebla Marriott about three miles down the *autopista*.

We were staying here, with or without a charge. I threw my MasterCard and Marriot Rewards number on the counter. It was time to solve this problem the American way, with money instead of bullshit. I gave the bellboy a big tip and told him I wanted to see the hotel maintenance man.

I showed the maintenance man, Antonio, the car, inducing a similar reaction as the day before. Tipping him, I explained, "*Necesito 240 voltios.*"

"No have," he said.

I spread my arms wide. "*Necesito 240 voltios.*" I pointed to the hotel. "*No 240 voltios, tres dias.*" I smiled and put my arm around his shoulder in a friendly gesture. "*Por favor.*"

He thought for a few seconds and then led me out on the hotel's lawn. There, he pointed to a socket. "*Doscientos cuarenta voltios.*"

"Dean," I said, bending over to look at the plug. "Will you go fetch my voltmeter?"

The socket was odd, but I thought I had something to rig it to the Tesla's adapter.

Dean arrived. The voltmeter read 240 volts. I quickly checked my electrical bag. I had the plug, but it was only rated for 20 amps. We'd get an 80 percent charge by ten the next morning. The only problem, the socket was more than a hundred yards from the car.

Dean and I ran our long extension cord literally through our hotel room (in the front door, out the back window) to make the distance. I rigged up the plug, checking all the leads with my voltmeter. We held our breath and plugged in the Tesla's adapter. Green. Whooh!

I gave Antonio a big hug. "*Muchas gracias.*"

• • •

That afternoon, as the car charged, I sat in the hotel room pondering the feasibility of the trip. Two of the previous four nights we only got a minimal charge, and in the two big cities we stayed, it had taken gargantuan, desperate efforts to find 240-volt power. Earlier in the day, before we had finally gotten the car plugged in, my stress level had peaked. Things were likely to get worse as we moved further south, into more rural and poorer areas.

For the first time since leaving Texas, I had genuine second thoughts. Was this whole venture possible? It was starting to look doubtful. A sense of gloom fell over me as I tried to put my emotions, now at a frenzy, aside and size up the future. Were there other alternatives? I spent two hours surfing the web for options to abandon or modify the trip. Possibly we could drive only to the Guatemala border, and then maybe back up to Cancun.

Yes, we had gone about eight hundred miles, but we'd brought a third of those miles with us by pre-charging the car. If we could get only 120-volt power every day, it would take us months to get to Panama. Worse, the power supplies that we'd found so far were not up to American standards, and the plug types were growing more rare and old.

I spent another couple of hours soul searching.

Before leaving, I heard the predictable discouragement from friends: This is not a good idea; you shouldn't go; don't get kidnapped; when you get somewhere cool like Costa Rica, I'll fly in; do you have a death wish? These things never worried me. My motivation was the challenge, and doing it in an electric car with limited range. Charging was the problem.

Failure at anything had always terrified me, especially public failure. It wasn't so much that I wanted to succeed as I didn't want to fail. But the sensible side of my brain said that we had bitten off too much.

Later that night, I told Dean I thought we should be prepared to modify our goals. Possibly he was as leery as I, but he put on his Army face, telling me what a baby I was (not in those terms), and reminding me of all we'd been through—that this was nothing.

"I got in that car with you when nobody else would," Dean said, his voice growing louder, "and I'll be *damned* if we're going to pack it in now. I'm supposed to be looking for a job. I'll push on without you if I have to. If we can't do it, we can't do it, but that's only after we actually can't do it, not just you *thinking* we can't do it. Quit being such a pussy."

Somehow, Dean's scolding eased my stress. I lit a Mexican cigarette and looked into his determined eyes. "Okay, we'll push on, feeling our way south, and see how things work out. But if I think we're getting into something that's not doable, we're stopping. We'll ship the car home."

As we argued, two hotel staff and the assistant manager showed up at our room. Two or three times during the day they had come to inspect the charging operation. I wasn't really sure what the problem was, but they didn't feel comfortable with us charging our car from their lone 240-volt socket on the hotel's back lawn. It didn't help that during the day, when we routed the cord, we accidentally set the charging rate to 30 amps—for a 20-amp socket! I don't know how we didn't blow a fuse (either the plug or the fuse was mis-wired!), but it must have shot their power meter up. I'd noticed the problem a couple hours earlier and lowered the charging rate to 14 amps.

The assistant manager, a young professional woman in her twenties who spoke some English, put a hand to her chin. "We think you should not charge the car tonight."

What now? I tried to think of a response to appease her.

Dean spoke up, confidently. "Electric cars are the new thing. Gringos will soon be pouring into Mexico in electric cars. The Marriott is a five-star hotel, and you need to be prepared and equipped for this if you're going to stay in business."

The assistant manager looked at Dean and then the car again. She seemed to buy his bullshit. "Okay, but we will keep a watch on it. But you will have to pay for the electricity."

"No problem," I answered. I think it was about 10:00 p.m. when the hotel staff left the room.

"See," Dean said, "it just takes a little can-do attitude."

I shrugged. "If I weren't such a high-flying Rewards member, they'd likely have pulled the plug on us. Maybe you *can* be a fat-cat and have the freedom."

Highway to Hell

The next morning, two-dozen German engineers dressed in expensive suits sat around the lobby of the Marriott discussing business very seriously. While I was checking out, the staff mumbled, trying to determine our cost for charging the car.

One of the clerks looked up at me and said, "Fifty dollars, American." I gladly paid.

It was 11:00 a.m.. We'd learned that it was best to wait until late morning for the fog to clear before making our descent through the mountain pass at Maltrada, so we decided to stay and let the car fully charge before departing Puebla.

I walked out to the hotel's portico and looked up at La Malinche, one of the three towering volcanoes encasing the city. Piercing the blue sky, its snow-covered apex turned steeply to the heavens. Named after Hernan Cortez's Indian mistress, whom the Mexicans still consider a traitor, the English translation of *La Malinche* is "Wicked Woman."

Below the mountain, the six-lane road hosted a modern traffic jumble, horns blasting away. Puebla, one of the country's original colonial cities, has a grand plaza and some of the most beautiful homes, squares, and elaborate churches in Mexico, including its cathedral, with fourteen chapels of various styles. It was here in 1862 where the Mexicans defeated the French on *Cinco de Mayo*.

And fifteen years earlier, during the Mexican-American War, the US Army occupied Puebla. The Mexicans undertook the siege of Puebla in an attempt to remove the Americans, ensconced in two forts on a hill a few miles away. The Mexicans cut the city's aqueducts. A testament to the city's antiquity sits behind the Marriott, a three-story-high portion of an old stone aqueduct, hidden away in a back alley and not important enough to be of any interest to anybody around here. We took a picture under its splendid, brown arches. Puebla was named a UNESCO World Heritage Site in 1987. Around the splendid Baroque and Spanish Renaissance architecture, a modern industrial city has developed, attracting major companies from around the world.

I would have loved to stay a few days to explore more of the city, but we were on the road to Veracruz and hopefully beyond by noon. I hadn't slept well the night before, but this morning, my worries again seemed to wane, and I was overtaken with the thrill of the trip and a newfound potency to give it our all. If we failed, we'd go down fighting. I could live with that.

Our route was along the oldest and most famous road in Mexico, Federal Highway 150, once called the National Road, built along the old overland trade route from the sea to the country's capital. Though the modern road deviated from the original route in places, it was along this general corridor that Cortez marched on Tenochtitlan, now Mexico City, from Veracruz five hundred years earlier.

Three hundred years later, General Winfield Scott and the American army used this path through the mountains to take Mexico City, all but ending the Mexican-American War after defeating the Mexican army at Cerro Gordo. That war resulted in the United States gaining possession from Mexico of Arizona, California, Nevada, New Mexico, and Utah, as well as portions of Colorado, Kansas, Oklahoma, and Wyoming.

The drive to the coastal plain took us from an elevation of 7,100 feet to sea level in a hundred miles. The early portion of the trip was dominated by the towering, snowcapped Orizaba Volcano, just off to our north, a jagged cone silhouetted against a cobalt sky and isolated from any apexes of significance. The volcano is the third highest peak in North America, at 18,491 feet, and the second tallest free-standing mountain in the world, behind Mount Kilimanjaro. I have climbed Kilimanjaro, but from the road, Orizaba looks like a much more daunting ascent, its upper slopes very steep.

• • •

The pass through Maltrada was a modern engineering marvel, the road descending more than three thousand feet in ten miles. Ahead, we saw the coastal plain over precipitous, almost vertical drops abutting the road that made my toes tingle. The big sky towered over the evergreen surrounds. Mystically, we rolled around sharp curves, down steep declines, over magnificent bridges, and through several tunnels, somehow getting closer to the little towns in the valleys below. The rollercoaster ride made me appreciate my profession and predecessors. Mexico's civil engineers originally pushed a railroad through these mountains in 1873.

Maybe all those days in a classroom studying subjects with intimidating names like thermodynamics or fluid mechanics (without an attractive women within a quarter mile of the classroom) had some benefits. There are a lot of words to describe engineering—tedious, thorough, precise, too serious—but descending the pass reminded me how lucky we are today. The men who built this road through the pass didn't have computers, calculators, or bulldozers.

With only pencil and paper, doing something as simple as calculating an inverse or raising something to a third root can be a major effort. Instead of pushing a few buttons, this work required pages of tables and calculations.

The modern engineering marvel below our butts loved the pass. The descent took no energy and actually added ten miles of range to the car. The Tesla Model S is equipped with a relatively new technology, regenerative braking. This allows the car's lithium-ion batteries to charge ever so slightly while braking or descending. Braking results in a huge loss of energy for all motorized vehicles, and piston-driven cars have no means to recapture it, so it's lost, grinding down the brake pads and tires. Regenerative braking captures and stores this often-wasted energy.

• • •

We spent the day trying to figure out how to best utilize the slopes and brakes to maximize our chances of reaching our goal tonight—a comfortable bed and a 240-volt socket. Finding the right mix was as much art as science.

In Cordoba, at the bottom of the pass, we pulled over, and I did a quick calculation. With the boost from the descent and at our current driving pace, we had enough battery power to travel almost 350 miles. Going over a few maps, we decided to bypass Veracruz and push on for the area in the mountains around Lake Catemaco that had a few tourist hotels. The total distance for the day would be about 225 miles, our best to date.

We moved onto the coastal plain, the ground now flat. We passed through fields of pineapple, orange, and something very familiar to Dean and me and our dear home in Louisiana—miles and miles of sugarcane. Better yet, now south of Veracruz, we had for the most part put the Mexican narcoworld safely behind us.

The Tesla's thermometer read eighty-seven degrees in January! The temperature had risen thirty degrees now that we were out of the mountains. Back in the States, the biggest story of the week was the deep freeze, the polar vortex descending on the country. Much of the Midwest and East Coast were below zero, and even in Louisiana, nightly temperatures dipped into the teens, closing schools.

The warm air rushing by and the desolate, rural setting perked up my spirits with renewed vigor. Only the night before, I was an emotional nutcase. Maybe I'm a fruitcake, on a perpetual Ferris wheel. I likely could find dozens of reputable citizens to attest to that. That's how I got in this mess in the first place.

As the day wore on, we went over a bunch of rivers, the first of any significance on the trip. First, we crossed the *Rio Papaloanplan* via its modern cable-stayed bridge, then the *Rio Tesechoacan*. The rivers worried me. I knew the complexities of crossing them in Latin America. When out of service, a surprisingly frequent occurrence, it might mean a day-long detour.

Late in the afternoon, I said, "This is the second day in a row without a *Federale* stop."

"Don't jinx us," Dean moaned.

I looked at the miles of sugar cane, the lime-colored stalks fluttering in the light wind. Black clouds of smoke from the burning after the harvest wafted over the fields of green, adding an urgent, busy ambiance, all so familiar to us. "From here on, the *Federales* will likely be the least of our worries."

I picked up the map. We'd covered almost 180 miles and still had almost 120 miles in the tank, but the easy part of the trip was now behind us. From here, rural, impoverished Chiapas and six Central American countries lay ahead. We'd be traveling for the most part off the tourist circuits, likely down bad roads with few western services.

As I scribbled some notes, Dean flashed his hazel eyes at me. "While you're jotting down that narrative, be sure to let your readers know this isn't a voyage of self-discovery for me, or a spiritual journey. It's just what I'm used to."

I continued to study the map. There were four possible towns in the next hour we could try to overnight in: Santiago Tuxtla, San Andres Tuxtla, Catemaco, and Acayucan. Only the latter was on the direct route, but services there seemed unlikely. The other three towns required a thirty-mile side trip to the east.

It was decision time. Until now, our route had been pretty straightforward, but henceforward we'd have to make choices. Which road to take or which town to shoot for? With our limited range at the end of the day, we'd unlikely have much room for error.

Another problem loomed, one we'd face daily as we bravely trudged on. How far should we push our range? If we found a town where we thought we could get a charge, but we still had seventy or eighty miles left in the tank, should we drive on? Over the course of the trip, fifty miles a day would add up to a lot of saved time, but if we got too intrepid, we faced the chance of ending up in the middle of nowhere, probably around dark. If we couldn't find a charge, we'd be stuck for no telling how long.

The first major decision of the sojourn reminded me that we were the masters of our domain. We weren't just plunging on with our fate predetermined. We were an integral part of the process that would determine if we passed or failed.

We neared the turnoff for Mexican Highway 179. The highway cut over to Catemaco directly, reducing our drive from a hundred miles to fifty. Our guidebook suggested we take the longer route.

"What do you think?" I asked.

Without hesitation, Dean said, "Let's do it."

The shadows growing long, we took off into the unknown. Let me say this now. If you're reading this book as a travel guide, do not take Highway 179. If you're a charged-up redneck in a souped-up 4x4 looking for fun, this is a hell of an adventure, but not in a Tesla that sits six inches—at best—off the ground.

Initially, the road wasn't that bad, asphalt with some large potholes. The only thing stirring my gut was the scenery, miles of sugarcane dotted with only a small farmhouse every couple of miles. As we ventured on, the road deteriorated, first to some type of hybrid gravel and asphalt, then to a dirt path filled with two-foot-deep potholes and blocked by washouts, where a hasty repair allowed one-way traffic.

In the shadows, we dodged more than fifty *topes*, dozens of chickens, horses, washouts, pedestrians, and even a couple of fanatical taxis. The potholes made anything in New Orleans seem like new airport runway.

Then came four bridges, if you want to call them bridges, each only wooden arches made of rough timbers lashed together and scalped back to the original piers after apparently being washed out. In the States, I wouldn't have walked across these bridges without making a personal inspection first, much less drive a two-and-a-half-ton car across them.

The road kept so much of Dean's attention, dodging obstacles, he didn't even film. Just in case, I grabbed the camera about thirty minutes down the highway.

We trudged along at maybe 15 mph for more than an hour. I cringed as the Tesla bumped along, its bottom scraping on the coarse gravel of the potholes or asphalt *topes*. My stomach tumbled, but the car just kept going. The sun started to dip below the horizon just as we climbed out of the delta and back into some small, tree-covered hills.

My heart jumped at the sight of two men ahead, standing on each side of the road. They held a flagged cable across the road, forcing us to stop. Were we about to be robbed? If they wanted the car, they should have taken it before we dragged it over all those potholes and bridges.

I looked back. Through the thick vegetation, I saw a few sprinkles of the lonesome valley behind us. Ahead, nothing but thick canopy—not even the hope of civilization or a man-made structure in sight. I didn't fancy turning around and driving back down HWY 179 in the darkness.

"What do you think?" Dean said in a hoarse voice, driving ahead cautiously.

Finally one of the men approached the driver's side, shouting some Spanish. Dean nudged the car forward, and I thought he might run through the hasty cable. Another man stepped in front of the car. Holy shit.

The first man came to Dean's window, putting two hands on the door. Middle-aged, dark, short, like a thousand other Mexicans we'd seen that week, he didn't appear hostile or armed. He belched some more Spanish.

My pulse pounding, I tried to understand his garbled words. Something about wanting money. "*Dinero*," I said. No problem, I've got plenty to give you.

"*Sí*," the man said, shoving his head further into Dean's window and continuing to babble.

A few tense seconds passed.

Dean looked at me. "Don't think they're robbing us.

But I think they're collecting money for something, maybe the road."

I turned to the man and spoke my best Spanish. "*¿Quieres algo de dinero para reparar el calle?*"

"*Sí, sí,*" the man said, his face still stern.

Relief fell over my entire body. "That's it. They want some money to fix the road."

"Pretty smart of them," Dean said, laughing.

The man returned the smile and backed away from the car.

I reached into the center console and handed the man all our change, probably fifty pesos. "Good idea," I said in Spanish as we rode off, still amused.

Somehow we made it. I'll give a prop to Goodyear and its nineteen-inch tires that survived all those treacherous potholes. First-class American craftsmanship, and we did appreciate it.

Under the setting sun, we passed through Santiago Tuxtla and San Andres Tuxtla. Our guidebook said cigars were made in the latter. No need to stop. I needed something stronger than a cigar. Just at dark, grooving to some Michael Jackson, we finally pulled into Catemaco and found an RV park and campground.

An elderly man had his RV backed up to a row of power outlets. I examined the sockets, 30-amp, 240-volt with a modern American plug. I looked over to some cabins for rent, but no one appeared to be at the campsite except the lone RVer.

I approached him. "You speak English?"

"Yes."

"You American?"

"German."

"Is someone here with the campground and RV park?"

"I think the owner's gone for the day."

"My car is electric. We need some of this power."

"Just plug it in," the man said, "and pitch here. You can settle up with the owner tomorrow. He seems like an agreeable fellow."

The park had cabins, but nobody to let us in. Darkness began to envelope everything. I didn't feel like camping after six hours on the road. If we were looking for adventure, we had found it.

As the last brushstrokes of sunlight painted the horizon, we rode through the small downtown and found a hotel with window AC units. The speed bump at its entrance was too big for the Tesla. We tried another hotel, a block over, the Hotel Playa Cristal. I quickly explained our situation to the friendly clerk, another Antonio, and he walked us behind the hotel to a secure, fenced-in parking area. He pointed to a 240-volt socket on the wall.

It couldn't be this easy. Dean pulled out our charging adapter as a few of the staff studied the strange car. Plugging it in, we got a green positive. I looked at the trip meter. We'd gone 234 miles today, the best day yet, but we were in the middle of nowhere with only about seventy miles of battery remaining. With 18-amp power, we'd be fully charged by noon the next day.

"How much?" I asked.

"Seven hundred and fifty pesos."

About fifty dollars. "We'll take it."

Topes and Potholes

The next day, waiting for the Tesla to be fully charged, we spent the morning exploring Catemaco, a tiny village 1,100 feet above sea level in the volcanic Tuxtla Mountains. Wedged beside Lake Catemaco, formed by a lava slide that created a natural dam in the high valley, the scenery was a nature lover's paradise. The unique volcanic belt abutted the coast. High rainfall and rich soil was something of an anomaly that created a biosphere of rainforest, coastal lagoons, and waterfalls—a haven for tree huggers and bird-watchers, but not much for road warriors on the hunt for easy 240-volt power, a bed, and a hot shower.

I had heard the village was famous for its witches with special powers to excise your internal demons. Maybe I could get some real and meaningful freedom—they could erase my memory, all forty-something years of it. I'd lose a few cherished moments, but on the whole, the pluses would outweigh the negatives. I asked at the hotel, but my inquiries resulted in no leads.

Checking out, I asked the hotel manager, a short, slender, middle-aged gentleman named Miguel, about HWY 179.

He mumbled and moaned, wringing his hands, his animated brown eyes wandering. "Huh, the worst of everything, the government and the San Juan River. We complain all the time, but they don't care about our little village, our way of life. We write letters, but they're tired of rebuilding it every year. The rich politicians in Mexico City don't give a damn about us."

"I'm starting to feel more at home every day. Mexico and America aren't that different," I replied, signing the ticket. I'd do my best to make sure that was the last river delta we'd see until returning to Louisiana.

We spent the morning strolling Catemaco's shaded, tranquil promenade populated with a few bars and restaurants, hastily slapped together along the waterfront but with great views of the lake and mountains. With tropical birds chirping and a fishy smell in our noses, we spied the decaying colonial architecture.

Just before noon, I sent some pictures and updates of our trip to Marcus Morton, a friend and movie producer in Santa Monica. Marcus was forwarding the updates to several other people who were tracking the trip, most notably, Mike Dunckley, an executive for several companies developing electric motorcycles, and through Mike, Bill Moore, who runs the webpage *EV World*. Bill stays on top of the latest news and developments in the electric vehicle industry. His webpage is one of the major hubs for industry professionals and EV enthusiasts looking for current information.

We still hadn't done enough to get *EV World*'s attention, or Bill to run a story, but with only a few more days of progress, people in the States would start to take notice. Marcus did send me a few brief questions in case he had some inquiries. One read: "What inspired you to take on this journey?"

I jotted a response without even thinking it over: "Just the challenge of it inspired me. Something like this has never been attempted. It's rare in 2014 to get to try something nobody has done." After sending it, I reread it a few times. It perfectly explained Dean's and my thoughts, at least initially.

Around noon, Dean stumbled into the room. "The car's charged. Let's get going."

"Just a second. Going over a few notes."

"Don't fret over that too much," Dean said. "Country-club Republicans like you don't do this type of stuff. That alone is a news story."

Shortly, we said goodbye to the affable staff at the Playa Cristal. Our goal today was Tuxtla Gutierrez, the capital of Chiapas, 240 miles down the road. There, we might find some better services. I needed to do some laundry. I was down to one set of clean clothes. The day before, my cell phone had quit. Maybe in Tuxtla Gutierrez I could get it reactivated?

I felt refreshed, having slept until eight-thirty. Except for the obligatory 3:00 a.m. rising to check the car's charge, the nine hours of sleep was my first elongated rest of the trip.

Due to our late arrival and the time required to charge the car, daylight had become our main problem. With the midday departures, we would likely run out of sunshine before battery. It wasn't advisable to drive in any country south of the border after dark, and I could only imagine the complexities of finding a charge in the darkness.

Having learned our lesson, we took the "good" road out of Catemaco. The one we should have taken the evening before. In the first hour alone, I counted thirty-four *topes*, three washouts that removed a lane from the road, and two cows in the road. Mexican potholes aren't like the American versions. If they're only four inches deep and two feet wide, you're lucky. Just like Louisiana during the harvest, sugarcane was scattered everywhere, and overloaded cane trucks drove wildly all over the place with complete disregard for anybody else.

The seemingly endless *topes* caused the most consternation for both me and the car. The constant decelerating and accelerating kills the car's range, then there were the unnerving winces as our batteries scraped over every ninth or tenth bump.

Catemaco and the Tuxtla mountains, now behind us, had all the trimmings of a nice little tourist trap where the locals could line their pockets with western currency from tourists and wacky environmentalists, if they'd just build a road there.

Finally we rolled through downtown Acayucan, *topes* city, and found a toll road. Whipping onto it, I spent the best pesos of my life as we accelerated to 45 mph, practically light speed. Moving onto the Tabasco Plain, we soon skirted around Minatitlan and then Coatzacoalcos, the latter the home of Salma Hayek.

From Coatzacoalcos, it was a 150-mile climb up to Tuxtla Gutierrez. Checking the vitals, we had about two hundred miles of battery, but only three and a half hours of daylight.

"Let's do it," Dean said.

I nodded and set the GPS. The road to Tuxtla Gutierrez was a big improvement. That is to say, it was paved and had no *topes*, but just to keep me from getting too gutsy, every few miles or so we crossed a pothole field. To my discontent, the potholes precluded sunglasses, necessitating hours of squinting. During the drive, dozens of foolish drivers passed us on all portions of the road, regardless of curves or hilltops. I wouldn't want to hold life or car insurance policies on any Mexican drivers.

· · ·

Twenty miles out of Coatzacoalcos, we passed over a somber landmark, one of the two railroads that connect Chiapas with the rest of Mexico and the United States. Known as the "Beast" or *Tren de la Muerte* (death train), these are the rails that Central Americans ride on their perilous, illegal trip to the land of milk and honey.

This rail leads to Tenosique, near the Guatemalan border. On a few occasions, I'd seen some migrants riding these trains, but nothing similar to recent images in the American press that depict hundreds of people clinging to boxcar roofs.

The sight must be jaw-dropping, a first-person view of the great twenty-first-century migration, like the mass Irish exodus west more than a hundred years ago. This movement by train is more akin to the early settlers' trek along the Oregon Trail across a lawless land, fraught with danger from fickle Nature and hostile Indians. But at least the pioneers had some organization, resources, and weapons.

In addition to the physical dangers, such as falling off the train, Mexico's darker elements ride the trains, robbing, murdering, and raping the defenseless migrants. Exact numbers are unknown, but estimates put the annual deaths from this arduous trip in the thousands. The Mexican authorities are often willing bystanders, if not participants. Two months after we crossed the Beast, several government officials were arrested for the torture and extortion of migrants during this very week in the Tenosique area.

Numerous local, international, and religious organizations have set up camps along these rails to house and feed these itinerants, offering some temporary shelter and protection. These groups have sometimes been harassed by the government and the gangs. Franciscan Fr. Tomás Gonzalez Castillo, who operates one of the camps in Chiapas and is a human rights activist for the migrants, has had death threats and been investigated by the federal government for human trafficking because of his relief efforts.

In recent years, several major Spanish-language films have been made about this human tragedy, two by major Hollywood production companies, but to date, most of the media attention has been in the Latin world, leaving most of our fellow citizens in the dark about the deadly consequences of reaching for the American dream.

· · ·

As we climbed up into the green mountains of Chiapas, I found the drive hypnotizing. The lush, verdant blanket of trees draped over the virgin hills, cool air, and gigantic views entranced me. The rugged mountains were a patchwork of green shades and unimaginable curves, especially with the sun shining from the side, all a rare experience.

When you're from Louisiana, hills of any sort are exotic. Much of the state is below sea level, and Mount Driskill, the tallest hill at an elevation of 575 feet, is so cloaked in thick forest that I've driven by it hundreds of times and never seen its peak. And when it comes to weather, Louisiana is rather plain, if not downright boring. With the exception of the brief seasonal transitions, the days are either miserably hot and steamy, or overcast and rainy, all lacking vivid hues and brisk, clean winds. When the wind does blow, it usually means it's about to rain cats and dogs.

As we plowed along, my restlessness started to ease. I'd even forgotten the day of the week. Time was dissolving. The Latin world lay ahead, without a plan, only a goal, and the trip had started to become a pleasant break from the world. Maybe I could relax and enjoy it? I hadn't had a vacation of any significance in five long years, the longest stretch of time in my life.

A couple of years earlier, my dear mother had passed away after a decade-long struggle with breast cancer. I assumed the role of her keeper for the last several years. Though spending so much time with her had been a gift, especially after years of separation since she sent me off to college with smiles and hopes, the additional time her care required and the trauma and chores involved with her death, had further complicated my miserable little life and kept my mind continuously buzzing.

One of the things I missed about Mom, especially as I was without a wife or kids, is not having anyone to make proud. A mother is the one person we never want to disappoint. Instead, mine was forever bragging on me, cutting out my newspaper clippings, or recording TV shows to show her friends. Since her passing, I had for some reason picked up a fondness for kids and little old ladies, going out of my way to give either a helping hand or friendly greeting.

I don't even know if I could've taken this trip while Mom was alive. A Southern drama queen, she would have worried constantly, and I would've likely been required to give her hourly updates on whereabouts and safety. Maybe she would have been a typical mother like Dean's, one of my favorites, who was actively, and likely continuously, tracking our progress via Dean's Facebook page that was now getting hundreds of views a day.

Thirty minutes before twilight we crossed the mountain reservoir of Netzahualcoyotl. Only forty-five more minutes to Tuxtla Gutierrez! I had been behind the wheel for more than five and a half hours and my eyes and mind yearned for a break. This wasn't like a scenic drive down the Pacific Highway. It was six hours of my devout attention, dodging gaping potholes, pedestrians, cows, and idiotic Mexican drivers. Certainly no place for dozing.

At dusk—just at the Mexican rush hour of 6:00 p.m.—we pulled into Tuxtla Gutierrez, sitting in a large valley in the Chiapas Mountains, its seven hundred thousand residents all seemingly trying to get home on the six-lane road we now traversed. At least I thought it was a six-lane road. It had no stripes, and the traffic varied from two cars wide to four cars wide on each side. Six lanes was only a good guess. We had succeeded again in our quest to leapfrog between population centers on our limited power. Our range down to about fifty miles, we were here until we found a charge, no matter what.

Through some internet research the night before, we had located a possible charging spot, the Hotel La Hacienda and RV Park. We found it without a wrong turn. Pulling in, I went through my now daily routine—lots of smoking, explaining, tips, questions, bartering, begging, and coaxing as the natives checked out the puzzling machine. The hotel manager led us to several rooms before we thought we had a charge point, a window unit with a 240-volt socket where we could pull the car to. We checked the voltage and plugged in the adapter. A green light!

An hour later, a call summoned me to the hotel's front desk. The owner wanted to see me. What now?

The old man, his hair departing and gray, his posture stooped, looked over a ledger and flashed his eyes at me.

The girl sitting beside him turned to face me. "You will have to pay for the extra electricity," she said in a dramatic tone, like she was informing me I had a fatal disease.

I didn't respond, saving myself the anguish, but reached into my front pocket and pulled out a half-inch wad of American bills. I flipped through them like a ticket scalper counting out change, all the while watching the old man's eyes. The bills got bigger as I continued to thumb.

The old man nodded at an exposed twenty.

With a flare of animation, I smirked, licked my thumb, pulled lose the twenty, plus an extra five, and set them on the counter, utterly enjoying the experience.

I didn't care. In the two days since I had considered abandoning the trip, we had gone 460 miles, more than I ever imagined or expected. Was it a coincidence that this had occurred once my aggravating cell phone had quit working, and I could finally concentrate on nothing but the trip? Was it Dean's General Patton pep talk a few days earlier? This was starting to look easy, but the Guatemalan border loomed only a day and a half away. Could we really pull this off?

Bouncing into the Clouds

We had another late departure the next day, the car not charged until noon. My only complaint with the Hotel La Hacienda: one side of my bed was six inches lower than the other. I'm sure the hotel manager didn't want to put us in the room, but it was the only one where we could get the car close enough to charge. To my satisfaction, the night before, I had my first American food of the trip: two large orders of French fries from the Burger King down the street.

Removing and replacing the battery on my cell phone got it working, and I passed the morning writing and returning a few emails. To my surprise, the phone didn't ring that morning and my email inbox was scant. Maybe everybody had finally determined I wasn't going to respond.

Dean surfed the internet, trying to plot our route as he bitched about my security protocols, leaving the door open every time I went to the car or left the hotel.

We didn't see much of Tuxtla, but it appeared clean and neat, its lights spanning miles across the huge valley at night. I had heard the city had a large indigenous population, but saw nothing discernibly different in the people, all friendly and helpful. There wasn't much to see in Tuxtla Gutierrez anyway, it being largely a transportation and administrative hub for Chiapas or for tourists heading to the ancient ruins of the powerful Maya: Palenque, Yax-chilán, Bonampak, and Chinkultic.

On our way out of town, we passed the international air-port, and I was reminded that I could quickly pull in and end this folly. Dean behind the wheel, we climbed up to San Cristóbal de Las Casas, forty miles away and five thousand vertical feet into the Sierra Madre de Chiapas Mountains. It was the toughest climb so far, consuming nearly a quarter of our battery.

Dean's personality generally doesn't fit the slow, conservative driving required to maximize the car's daily range. That is, he likes to drive aggressively. Not recklessly, but with a lot of accelerating and decelerating, which consumes more power. It's hard to blame him, as the Tesla Model S is intoxicating to drive. It's one of the fast-est factory cars in America. Despite its benign appearance, it can go zero to sixty in 5.6 seconds, and will pull your cheeks back just passing somebody on the interstate. The Tesla is built to drive fast and also has a five-star crash safety rating, one of the best on the road, but due to its spunk, I suspect it can induce dangerous driv-ing. It's certainly easier to burn power in the car than it is to replace it, especially in these parts.

Understandably, any two people that spend all day together in a car, and then are forced to bunk together, will be sick and tired of each other after a week. So at the top of the San Cristóbal pass, Dean wanted to stop and take a picture. I didn't object, but instead of pulling just off the road, he motored beside an old debris pile where someone had dumped a bunch of concrete, flush with form-ing boards, nails, and rebar.

When I said something about it, he got all stirred up and yelled. "You drive if you don't like the way I drive! You're being so damn conservative and worried, you're ruining the trip."

"Hell, yeah," I said under my breath. "We're in the middle of Chiapas. We don't know a soul. I barely speak the language and you don't at all."

I took over the driving. Both of our nerves were frayed from the long days, the unknown, and the general discomfort of being in such an isolated spot with no friends or support.

I drove on into the clouds and around the edge of San Cristóbal. When the fog broke, the land revealed itself as a wonderful alpine world, the towering slopes thick with pine. We passed through five or six tiny hamlets, minuscule collections of woodsheds and a few lean-tos around a dirt plaza with maybe a brick well along the highway. The short, tan natives walked along the shoulders or gathered near the bus stop. Likely, nothing has changed in these villages for decades.

We rolled over *topes* galore. I don't know how many, fifty, seventy-five, one hundred, probably closer to the latter. On four or five occasions, we scraped over the speed bumps. How much more pounding could the batteries take? The Model S weighs almost 4,700 pounds, without us and our gear, extremely heavy for a car its size. A Corvette, for example, only weighs 3,200 pounds.

By midafternoon, the fog returned, this time much worse. Visibility was reduced to thirty feet on the tight, mountain road without shoulders. It was so bad, even the locals wouldn't pass. As I drove along, white-knuckles grasping the steering wheel, I feared a dumbass barreling around a curve, or one of the cows we'd seen earlier that day walking in the road. We'd likely collide with either before we saw them. I hit one *tope* without a sign at maybe 20 mph. My heart jumped into my throat, but we dodged a bullet. The obstacle was small, just a bump instead of the bone-jarring collision I feared.

I can't speak for all of America, but there is no way Louisian-ans would tolerate all these speed bumps. They'd be out in the road with their own backhoes and dozers removing the damn things, drinking beer, and likely putting the concrete rubble they scraped up to good use, touching up the shoulders on their driveways or building new roads to their deer hunting camps.

We finally made the ninety miles to Comitán, the last town of any size before the Guatemalan border, in just over three hours. At this pace, batteries wouldn't be our problem. It would take ten to twelve hours to expend our daily range. We planned to stay here for the night as we'd been told to cross the border as early in the day as possible.

In town, we cruised the main drag a few times, looking for a charging point. We stopped at one thirty-dollar-a-night hotel with-out luck. We then headed for the congested city center. There, we parked and Dean and I took off in opposite directions, canvassing the area on foot for possible charging points. This went on almost two hours. It was something like a comic opera, the residents won-dering who the white-faced lunatics were who kept pacing around from hotel to hotel on some arcane business. Complicating this, Dean didn't have a cell phone. We decided to meet back at the car if we found something, which we didn't.

Coming to grips with the fact that we'd probably only get a par-tial charge this evening, we stumbled on another hotel, the Hotel Lagos de Montebello, a fifty-dollar-a-night establishment. I went in and explained our situation. The hotel bellboy led us around back to a few old sockets against the back fence. They looked like they hadn't been used in years and also had an unusual design, but they were 240 volts and I thought I had an appropriate adapter. My volt-meter told me no power, but we got the bellboy to find the breaker and turn them on. The power restored, my voltmeter read 240.

The adapter was a little more complicated. I wasn't familiar with it, but had picked it up somewhere and thrown it in my plug bag, and hadn't ever wired it.

We cut the power and went to work putting the plug together. My first attempt at wiring didn't give us a green light on the Tesla's adapter. We cut the power again, and I rewired the plug, double-checking the two positive leads. Two-hundred-and-forty volt power is not something to mess around with. It can kill you quickly.

We plugged everything up and got the bellboy to flip the power back on. I held my breath. The voltmeter read positive, and just a few seconds later the Tesla adapter went green. Success! We were hooked up to 240-volt, 18-amp power. The car would be fully charged in ten hours.

The hotel manager arrived at the spectacle, and he and the bellboy discussed something I didn't understand.

The manager then spoke up. "There will be a fee for electricity," or something like that.

The two hotel employees then conversed and bickered for another thirty seconds. Shoulders shrugged. Both men mumbled. The manager scratched his black hair and then turned to me. "Cost to charge is 150 pesos."

Eleven dollars. One thing was for sure—in Mexico, the price for charging, even if extorted, was highly variable!

Stranded by a Snowstorm

The next morning we were poised to cross the border into Guatemala but had a small snag. Some paperwork and insurance that I needed to drive in Guatemala had not arrived in my inbox. AIG had agreed to provide this service for a fee. All had been finalized a few days earlier, but now, waiting to cross the border, the paperwork hadn't materialized.

I got on the phone with the agent in Brownsville. He gave me a story that AIG's office, somewhere in the northeast, was closed due to a major storm.

Dude, we crossed deserts, mountains, and jungles on third-world roads to get here, scrounging around for power on a makeshift electrical grid, and these guys were going to hold us up over some storm? No wonder the Feds had to bail out AIG. Market forces should probably have been allowed to end this incompetence.

After a few emails and five or six phone calls, I finally got the paperwork, but it was after lunch, too late to depart for the day, especially since we'd only averaged 30 mph the day before. Our next destination was, hopefully, Lake Atitlán, 150 miles into Guatemala, and we had to cross the border.

Moderating our urge to push on, we met a young man at the hotel who spoke excellent English. He told us to only travel in

Guatemala during the daylight, and make sure we had an adequate place to stay by late afternoon. We were stranded for the day.

The good news was that Comitán appeared to be a jewel hidden at 5,400 feet in the Chiapas Mountains. The alpine paradise was a popular vacation spot for Mexicans. It had blue skies, warm days, cool nights, and beautiful vistas. Filled with tight, hilly streets (a little like Pacific Heights in San Francisco), colonial buildings, smiling faces, and a lively plaza, money didn't appear to be God here. We'd seen a few European tourists, but not one American. The kids' big, curious, brown eyes stared at Dean's strange green eyes and my auburn hair. We were foreigners in their backyard.

When abroad, I often try to discern America's effect on the people and landscape. Even here, it was everywhere. Three or four car dealerships sold American brands. There was a Walmart, Domino's, Burger King, and Autozone. In the *centro*, the droves of young people bounced around on Nikes, babbling away on their cell phones and tapping on iPads as they ducked in and out of the numerous internet cafes.

In my touring of Latin America, I've found that it is best to stay ahead of the loud, rampaging *Norte Americanos*, ever thrusting out from their borders. Their arrival, en masse, can turn a pleasant beach or mountain retreat into something more akin to a Spanish Bourbon Street. Which means you always have to keep exploring and moving to stay in front. It seems that the advent of the information age has reduced the trailing time of the invaders so much that if you find a little special place in 2014, you'll likely never see that place again, especially if there's an international airport within an hour's drive. Hopefully for us, driving might extend this post-discovery time by a few more years when we found something like Comitán.

• • •

I remember my first experience in Costa Rica years ago on a fishing trip. On our way out of the country, we decided to give San José, the capital, a try. Our guidebook recommended the Blue Marlin Sports Bar and Hotel Del Rey, citing the place as popular with "sportsmen and prostitutes." This was not a guidebook you'd buy at Walmart or your neighborhood bookstore, but something I'd picked up at a Costa Rican truck stop.

I'm strictly a sportsman, but I may have possibly traveled with some friends who might be interested in the other aspects of the hotel. Anyway, the place turned out to be a real treat. Part hotel, part bar, part casino, and part house of ill repute, it had good rooms for fifty dollars—a nice family-run establishment. We had a terrific dinner at the hotel, and afterward in the bar, discussed fishing as we took in the spectacle of probably seventy-five attractive, polite working girls mingling with maybe a dozen sportsmen. The gaudy, in-your-face nature of the place and ratio of women to sportsmen kind of made the hotel a sightseeing stop.

It was a gringo dream, a place so unique and outlandish, someone could bring their devout Baptist dad in and he'd get a kick out of it. We were treated like true kings for a day. I told one of my fishing pals on the way to the airport, "If the gringo ever discovers the Blue Marlin Sports Bar, they'll have to add a half-dozen more daily flights from Dallas to San José."

Sure enough, some years later, maybe five, maybe ten (I'm getting so old it all runs together now) I was back in Costa Rica fishing. On our way out of the country, I told the guys, "I've got to take you by this place in San Jose the night before we depart. You've never seen anything like this."

The night before we departed I motored up to the Blue Marlin and walked inside to get a couple of rooms. I was quickly told the joint was not only full, but they were full for the next thirty days. The board behind the counter indicated that the price for rooms, if available, was north of $100 a night. To make matters worse, it looked like everything in the area was getting remodeled. I looked over my shoulder to the bar that had been somewhat tranquil a few years earlier. The free market reigned, and the hotel and casino looked like some type of Latin, X-rated Disneyland. More than a hundred Americans, flashing their money, had wedged themselves into the bar that an American fire marshal would have rated for no more than forty.

• • •

Anyway, we'd found a little treasure in southern Mexico, and we'd enjoy it before the strip malls went up—or worse, oil was discovered nearby.

I spent the free day wandering around Comitán's rolling streets and *zocalo,* and took care of a few pressing items back home.

Late that evening, I put the Tesla back on charge. We planned to be on the road early, six-ish. How far would we make it into Guatemala after we crossed the border? At the pace we made the day before, it would likely take eight hours to get to our first possible place to overnight, but the road might be worse. For certain, it promised to be hilly and winding.

Dean again found the Louisiana Tech basketball game on his Chinese website. It didn't get my mind off the daunting task at hand—six more countries to cross. In the next twenty-four hours we'd find out a lot about ourselves, and the viability of our long-term goals.

Land of the Maya

Early the next morning, the eastern sky shifting from indigo to crimson, we finally rolled out of Comitán. It was about fifty-five miles to the Guatemalan border. Not far out of town, civilization vanished as we darted up and down, round and round, here and there, over the *topes,* and slicing through the green hills. Most of the *topes* were designed for their intended purpose, to slow traffic instead of rip off the car's suspension, but in one little hamlet the regional road engineer must have had a sadistic side.

The endless jade hills of Chiapas are one of the most impoverished and lightly populated areas in Mexico. Here, the people are more indigenous than Mexican, and as likely to speak a local dialect as Spanish. Due to its rugged mountains, and lack of mineral riches or rich farmland, Chiapas has been a remote backwater for five hundred years.

• • •

This is the home of the left-wing, anti-Mexican Zapatista Army of National Liberation. Though it has been almost twenty years since the rebels' last major uprising, the movement still flexes its muscle occasionally, and frequently feuds with the federal government. In the last two decades, Mexico City has given the region more attention and resources, but any peace is fragile. To date, the rebels have yet to sign a peace treaty with Mexico City, and in recent years, most of the regional unrest has moved to Oaxaca, one state to the north.

• • •

Western services outside of the major towns are rare here, and while living in the adjacent state of Campeche, I felt concern as I traveled these roads, even with native Mexicans, a decade earlier. Today, like then, my worries weren't the revolutionaries but just the sheer isolation of the place, a huge no-man's-land in the harsh mountains between the towns. Early in the day, we passed only a few cars.

I couldn't help but fret about a mishap here, a mechanical problem or a slide off the road. I didn't relish the thought of overnighting in this bush.

It's not that I fear Mexicans, or sleeping on the side of the road. I have bunked under the stars in plenty of strange places in Louisiana, and I have no doubt Mexicans are no more nefarious than Louisianans.

Actually, I'm quite certain average Mexicans are much less threatening than average Louisianans. But in Louisiana, any potential perpetrator has to worry that the intended victim is packing a high-caliber firearm and would love to get some practice on a live target. In Mexico, only bad guys have guns so they are less inclined to be cautious with strangers.

For the first time, the euphoria of the trip had started to subside. Both Dean and I were now mostly engaged in the business of getting there. We were somewhat like Lewis and Clark, traversing the unknown, trying not to get lost, fleeced, or stranded. Where Lewis and Clark daily searched for water and shelter, trying to avoid hostile Indians, we looked for 240-volt outlets with easy access to the road, internet service, possibly some nightlife, and cozy, comfortable beds.

As we approached the Guatemalan border town of La Mesilla, I scanned the scenery for archeological ruins. I remembered my frequent traipsing of the rural roads on the Yucatan Peninsula, where I would pass old ruins or smaller pyramids grown up in the brush and seemingly unexcavated beside the road. To my disappointment, here in Chiapas I saw nothing.

Nerves in my spine tingled as we passed through La Mesilla and then through the two-mile neutral zone between Mexico and Guatemala. The first Guatemalan border guard we encountered asked for our papers, studied them briefly, and then told us we had to turn around and go back to Mexico to get processed out of the country before we could go on to Guatemala.

This perplexed me as I didn't know you ever had to be "let out" of a country. When we left the States, the US border guards stopped us only to make sure we knew we were headed to Mexico.

We turned around and drove back the two miles. There, Mexican immigration and customs stamped us out of the country. There was a third stop, to sign some papers so I would get my four hundred dollars back that I'd paid to drive into Mexico.

Assured that we could now proceed, we drove back to the Guatemalan border and were welcomed into the country by a speed bump so huge I wasn't sure we could even scrape across it.

The other side of the border was a maze of chaos. Tens if not hundreds of hasty shacks had been erected adjacent to the narrow road, selling anything and everything, and hundreds of people filled the street. It looked like we were about to drive through a county fair in Ohio.

We began the confusing, problematic, bureaucratic process that would forever haunt us while moving south through six Central American countries, getting ourselves, and more importantly, the car through customs and immigration, and obtaining drivers' permits.

Immigration was pretty straightforward: a ten-minute wait in line and a stamp. Then the car was fumigated. After it was sprayed, I was given a receipt in exchange for one American dollar, and the border guard pointed to a little building with a sign over the door: *Aduana.*

Through the building's open window I presented my passport to the customs agent on duty. "*Buenos días señor. Tengo un coche, pero mi español es muy malo.*"

The tall, slender man squinted, producing an unpleasant face. "*Su problema.*"

Translation: "It's *your* problem you don't speak Spanish."

I pushed forward all my paperwork, my Mexican car permit, proof of insurance, driver's license, car registration, title, bill of sale, and some other documents Mexican customs had given me upon our exit. This initiated a thirty-minute process in which I filled out several more pieces of paper. Documents were looked over and copied, and some simple verbal exchanges were attempted. The crux of the process required that I get a Guatemalan driver's permit and the car be cleared through customs.

The mystifying, lengthy procedure went on for almost an hour until the customs agent grabbed a stack of papers and walked outside to inspect the car.

While I'd been inside worrying and explaining, Dean had been conversing with the immigration and customs agents, and a dozen or so natives all now stood around the car, its trunk and hood open. They all seemed amazed that the car didn't have a motor.

Dean had pulled out the charging adapter and was demonstrating how we charged the car.

Several of the officials were sitting in the car, and a few more were having their pictures taken in front of it.

The scene lightened the custom agent's mood, and he only briefly looked over our belongings before signing our paperwork and sending us on with well wishes. I looked at my watch. It was now 10:00 a.m.. The border crossing had taken about an hour and a half. Two border crossings down. The process had been so cumbersome and time-consuming that we decided we didn't have the time to get Dean a driver's permit, which was fine with me.

As we pulled away from the customs house, we were assaulted by money changers and peddlers. I exchanged a Ben Franklin for Guatemalan quetzals, but we were going nowhere. A quarter mile up the road, an 18-wheeler had tried to turn around on the tight street, producing a twenty-car line. People screamed and bitched. Horns blared. The local police stormed into the mess in hopes of sorting everything out. The truck was wedged sideways, the cab facing a vertical hill. It would be a while before the cops could get the truck back on the road and out of the way. Over the road, a huge sign read: *Bienvenido a Guatemala.*

Crazy Drivers, Big Mountains

*F*rommer's *Travel Guide* says this about driving in Guatemala:

> In general, I don't recommend renting a car in Gua-
> temala. The roads are often dangerous. Guatemalan
> drivers, particularly bus and truck drivers, have appar-
> ently no concern for human life, their own or anybody
> else's. A brutal Darwinian survival of the fittest reigns on
> Guatemala's roads. Passing on blind curves seems to be
> the national sport. Pedestrians, horses, dogs, and other
> obstacles seem to appear out of nowhere.

It didn't take long driving up and down the twisting road to determine that *Frommer's* had a good handle on driving in Guatemala.
Despite this, I couldn't help but be overwhelmed by the beautiful
country, the most mountainous terrain we had yet crossed. Even
in the twenty-first century, railroads have not penetrated the steep
mountains of Guatemala's western highlands.

We entered the country into one of the most impressive,
majestic valleys I'd ever seen. The steep, teal slopes fell almost

vertically thousands of feet from a royal blue sky to a narrow gully
barely wide enough for the road to squeeze beside a clear, blue
mountain river filled with raging rapids. The tight, winding road,
steep drop-offs, and drivers racing and passing caused me to redis-
cover religion more than a few times.

In the first hour, we were stopped twice by the police. The first
was almost by accident when a senseless Guatemalan driver passed
us on a sharp curve. Just for good measure, the *policía*, armed with
machine guns, waved us in with the mad driver. The officer ques-
tioned me for five or ten minutes.

Translation: "Why don't you have a Guatemalan driver's
license?"

I produced the permit I'd just spent over an hour laboriously
getting. Just when I was starting to get worried, a soldier arrived,
dressed in green camouflage. After some lengthy conversation with
the policeman, they let us go.

The second stop was the more conventional, American version, the cops rushing up behind us with flashing lights. This one
went a little quicker. We told them we were tourists and showed
them the electric car and all our charging cords, etc. They laughed
a little and let us go.

Guatemala, the most populous and fastest-growing country
in Central America, is in transition. With almost 40 percent of its
people indigenous and its per-capita income only about a third of
Mexico's, it has only recently begun to recover from its more than
thirty-year civil war that ended in 1996. Most of the war, waged
between the right-wing government and the rural poor, primarily
ethnic Mayan and Mestizo peasants, transpired outside our windows in the western highlands.

Twentieth-century Central America is filled with bloodshed
and strife—civil wars, revolutions, proxy wars, rich versus poor,

urban versus rural, establishment against progressive, East against West—but nowhere was the exploitation and subjugation of the indigenous people more brutal than in this country.

The story of Guatemala's Maya and their struggle for equality is long and complex. Rigoberta Menchú, an indigenous woman from the western highlands, wrote a bestselling story of her life as she rose from a young peasant worker to become a leading human-rights voice for the region's indigenous people. Most of her family were killed by government forces along the way.

In 1992, she was awarded the Nobel Peace Prize, one of only three Central American Nobel laureates. There is also an award-winning documentary about Rigoberta's story, *When the Mountains Tremble.*

In the last decade, *La Violencia,* as the Guatemalans call it, has settled down, but scuffles, some resulting in death, still continue between the liberals and the police, and of course, the drug lords utilize the area to move their precious merchandise closer to the market—upscale America.

• • •

As we drove on, stopping several times for traffic to be diverted onto gravel paths around washouts, I fretted, continuously staring at the range meter. It didn't take long to determine this was coffee country, and it must have been the harvest season as the truck beds were loaded with either workers headed to the fields or bags of the valuable harvest. Along the road, coffee bags were stacked ten feet high.

The road kept climbing, our pace excruciatingly slow over the *topes,* now call *tumulos* (most designed much better than the Mexican versions), around three-wheeled taxis darting everywhere, and enterprising capitalists standing on the edge of the road shoving papaya, melons, and nuts into our window. I appreciated their entrepreneurial spirit, but weaving around them took my full attention. At every little village, our pace slowed even more as big trucks wedged onto the road from everywhere.

For some time, we followed an old Guatemalan bus and got to watch two of the bus's employees climb back and forth between the bus's roof and passenger bay through the back door—while the bus drove, bouncing over the terrible road! I backed away for fear that if one of the workers fell, we might run over him.

In Guatemala, like most of Central America, buses are the primary means of transportation for most people, and fill the roads, overcrowded with smiling faces, and constantly stopping and starting. They range from a few modern models similar to Greyhounds to the more frequent versions, called chicken buses, the standard American yellow school bus, some probably sold south of the border by the East Baton Rouge School District twenty years earlier after they were worn out and deemed unfit for transporting kids across the parish.

Here, they're given a fresh coat of paint, not yellow, but loud colors, psychedelically displayed without order and adorned with weird murals, obviously painted by some artist unable to make a living on canvas. By my inspection, a single rule governs the chicken buses: there's always room for one more!

• • •

Since Tuxtla Gutiérrez, we had been on the Pan American Highway, built in the 1930s to connect Alaska with the southern tip of South America. The road's name evokes a major public-works project. Don't be fooled. Likely, the project was some type of scandal that lined the pockets of contractors or government officials across two continents. Much of it resembles an unmaintained, rural county road in America, except here, it traverses one of the roughest mountain ranges in the hemisphere.

By late morning, our range down to about a hundred miles, I worried that we had made a wrong turn somewhere. For most of the morning the river that paralleled the road had been flowing against our direction of travel, but now the water ran with us and had been doing so for more than thirty minutes. I'm a civil engineer by profession, but it doesn't take an expert to know that water in any river doesn't turn around and flow upstream.

Dean needed to relieve himself, so I pulled over and whipped out our only hard-copy map of Central America. Fortunately, the three-foot by three-foot piece of paper was both a road and topographic map. I quickly determined that through the morning we had climbed up the Selegua River valley, but somewhere, the road crossed the continental divide, over the 10,000-foot-high Cordillera de los Cuchumatanes Mountains, and there, the pass formed the headwaters of two rivers, the Selegua, and the Rio Sacuma, which flowed south. I touched a button on the Tesla's range meter that graphically displays the average energy usage for the last thirty miles. It clearly lets the driver know if he has been ascending or descending. Relief filled my soul as I realized we had been driving downhill for the last fifteen.

By two-thirty, after eight hours on the road, we had traveled all of 150 miles, but then stumbled on a miracle—a patch of new, four-lane road.

Forty minutes later, we approached the turnoff to Panajachel. We had a tip. Panajachel had a hotel owned by a pair of Americans. It was about 3:00 p.m., and we had seventy-one miles left in the batteries. Another decision.

We opted for the conservative path and turned off to Pana-jachel, immediately commencing a precipitous descent. I pulled over to check the map again, always leery that we might end up at the bottom of a valley and be forced to climb back out of it with lit-tle spare power. It was nine miles to Panajachel, 3,000 feet below us.

We slogged on, down the winding road, through the town of Solola and its pedestrian market, the brick road jammed with peo-ple, animals, motorcycles, and vehicles of every make, until we got our first glimpse of the impossibly beautiful Lake Atitlán, a won-derful sheet of water stretching for miles to the horizon, glistening, encased by towering green volcanoes, and draped over a mountain caldera.

I glanced at my watch and the odometer. It had taken us more than nine hours to make today's two hundred-mile trip. Even dis-counting the time spent crossing the border, we had averaged a measly 28 mph. At this rate, how long would this trip take?

But we would make it and, more importantly, we had made it well into Guatemala, in an electric car! Euphoria filled me. How far could we go? Could we possibly succeed? We still had six coun-tries to cross, all considerably more difficult than Mexico, and we still needed to find a charge today. Thus far, the adventure usually began when we reached our daily destination.

The Car Steals the Show

O n the outskirts of Panajachel we saw a sign for the Hotel Atitlán, the hotel we'd heard was owned by two Americans. We pulled in, but to our disappointment, the security guard told us they had no vacancies. Next door sat the Hotel Bahia del Largo. I went in and explained our situation. In no time, I was walking the hotel with the very polite clerk and one of the hotel's maintenance men, both intrigued by our situation.

After fifteen minutes of looking, we found no 240-volt power at the hotel, but at the hotel's adjacent event center, we found a dryer and GE electric stove. I checked the dryer's outlet, only 120 volts, but removing a few drawers next to the stove, we checked the connection, a modern NEMA 240-volt, 30-amp socket. My voltmeter said it was good, and we soon pulled the car to the event center and stretched one of our extension cords into its kitchen. We were charging at 26 amps, my best charge of the trip. We'd have a full charge by four in the morning.

By the time we got the car rigged up to charge, most of the hotel staff and the manager had showed up to look at the Tesla, amazed we'd driven it from America. In no time, most everybody was taking pictures of the car and treating us like celebrities.

After checking in, I ambled over to our room and saw four of the hotel staff, to my disapproval, hand-washing the Tesla. The dust-covered car needed a bath, and I appreciated the generosity, but I liked the car dirty. Covered in grime, it didn't look that expensive or appetizing for bandits. With the custom washing, it now looked like it had some value and would attract attention.

Somewhere along the road, we'd transitioned from *loco gringos* into sensations, but the car was the real star of the show. With two countries and thousands of potholes and speed bumps in our rear-view mirror, the little, amazing electric car looked no worse for wear. There's a simplicity, and with it, a reliability in electric transportation, an evolution similar to replacing piston-driven airplane engines with jets—performance not only increases, but so does the dependability due to the lack of moving parts.

• • •

Electric cars have very little that can break down or require maintenance. They have no transmission, carburetor, fuel or water pumps, alternator, radiator, starter, power steering pump, or spark plugs, to name just a few components, and none of the belts, oils, and filters required by these support mechanisms. Electric cars only have batteries that power the simple electric motor and its supports. Like a ceiling fan, they run seemingly forever with nothing to break down.

The lack of moving parts produces pure power, straight from the electric motor to the wheels without being routed through a transfer case and transmission, and without having the burden of running all the other mechanical devices. And it has no exhaust that can contaminate the air, especially in the third world, where the cities are extremely dense, and cars and trucks often belch a continuous stream of thick, gray smoke.

Founded by American engineers Martin Eberhard and Marc Tarpenning, Tesla Motors was incorporated in 2003. A year later, South African Elon Musk led a major investment into the company and became chairman of its board. A graduate of the University of Pennsylvania with degrees in economics and physics, and a co-founder of PayPal, an online financial services company, Musk has since been the face and driving force behind Tesla, taking over as CEO in 2008.

The Palo Alto, California-based company struggled early. From 2006 through 2012, it sold only about 2,500 of its sole model, the Roadster, a two-seat sports car priced at just over 100,000 dollars. But Tesla succeeded where all the world's major car manufacturers had failed. It put a reliable electric car on the road. The key selling point, lacked by its competitors, was the Roadster's lithium-ion battery cells that provided a practical range of over two hundred miles under typical driving conditions.

In 2010, the company made its initial public offering, the first American car company to go public since the Ford Motor Company in 1956. Musk's stated goal was to bring affordable, practical, electric cars to the masses. In the years since, the price of a share has increased tenfold, and in 2012 the four-door Tesla Model S hit the streets. In its first year and half on the market, Tesla sold more than 25,000 units of the Model S.

The current price of a new Model S: somewhere between 70,000 and 105,000 dollars, depending on features and battery capacity. In Louisiana, the car's biggest plus is that it cost about seven dollars in electricity to go 265 miles. If you live in some

Democratic stronghold like California or New York, where electricity is much more expensive, double this.

• • •

Due to their simplicity, with time and scale, the cost of electric cars will shrink significantly below conventional gasoline-powered cars or trucks. I base my opinion of electric cars on the best available information. The facts are clear: electric motorization is a more efficient, cost-effective means of transportation than gas or diesel vehicles. Much more importantly, we can power these cars with American electricity produced from domestic energy.

I worked in the oil industry for years. Today, with much of Asia starting to drive, we're burning oil at levels unimaginable only thirty years ago, with current consumption quantities outpacing discovery rates.

The wonderful age of oil is ending. In the long run, the price will only climb higher and higher, the reserves located in more and more complicated places. We buy more than 200 billion dollars of foreign oil every year. That's not to mention the billions we spend every year guarding the overseas supplies. Without oil, there never would have been an Osama Bin Laden, and the loss of all the blood and treasure trying to stymie the next big terrorist.

If you lack the aptitude to decipher the magnitude of these billions and trillions, let's just say it's enough money to solve any of America's pressing problems, with plenty left over. A solution to our reliance on oil will have to come at some point, and when it does, the entities, companies, and countries that have the technology to keep producing goods and services without oil will command the power and wealth. I vote for the same nation that solved most the world's problems in the last century. Still, electric cars and Tesla are not completely out of the woods. Elon Musk, having invested almost his entire fortune in the car company, nearly lost it all in 2008 when the company's finances verged on the perilous. Even today, though Tesla's stock has soared and the company is valued at over 30 billion dollars, it has yet to show a profit.

It will take years of hard work, research, and billions of dollars invested in the basic electrical infrastructure needed to charge electric cars before they're fully incorporated into the mainstream.

Southern Summer of Love

The car in good hands, Dean and I headed into town. Now late in the afternoon, I noticed for the first time that the days had started to grow longer, probably by an hour. This made me ponder the enormity of the distance we'd traveled, now about 1,500 miles.

I found Panajachel charming, one of several Mayan villages around the lake. We strolled down the *Calle Santander,* an open-air market. Latinos and indigenous Mayans sold Western comforts and all sort of Mayan collectibles to the hundreds of tourists wedged between the shops, restaurants, and bars. More tourists paced the town than we'd seen cumulatively the entire trip.

There were a few retiree types and backpackers, but mostly the town resembled some type of American college-aged hippie-fest, the youth of the world's most powerful country stumbling around in sandals, stringy hair, generally showing off their free spirits. I even smelled pot a few times.

I've never smoked a joint, mostly because since I reached the age of consent, I've been subjected to perpetual drug tests, either by the US Army or my profession, but I can roll with almost anything. I generally subscribe to the live and let live approach.

Part of my love for all things outside of America is the disorder, the lack of rules, the independence. Despite its greatness and economic power, America is becoming a bland place of uniformity. Though I'm certain it was once the most interesting spot on the planet, the media and federal government's never-ending war to make us all homogeneous is bearing fruit. They're standardizing us in the name of political correctness.

My dear home, Louisiana, the closest thing left in the United States to something truly unique, has resisted this for decades, but I fear we're like the last house surrounded by a spreading wildfire. Just last fall, I was informed there was no smoking in the piano bar at Pat O'Brien's in New Orleans. Appalled, I inquired about this aberration, as I know well New Orleans will be the last place in America to put aside man's unhealthy pleasures. The waiter replied, "Go to the patio bar if you want to smoke. Most of the tourists don't like smoke."

Hell, that defeats the entire purpose of the place. Louisiana has not a single natural wonder, not even a beach, but the tourists flock in to enjoy our culture, our festivals, our madness, and our incredibly diverse and interesting people. Individualism reigns supreme. If someone wants to go out for a night where everyone dresses and behaves the same, and they're told what to do, they'll stay in St. Louis. I fear that, in another generation, Louisiana will be more like Iowa than Bohemia, forced to conform, and that we will lose all local flavor.

We Americans have by and large fallen for this hoax. We adore certainty, abhor chance, snub unconventionality. Americans transformed a virgin continent into the world's most powerful country in less than two centuries primarily due to our rejection of Old World rules and rituals, accomplishing things other countries couldn't even dare to dream. Now it seems we're taught to obey and follow, rest on our laurels.

• • •

As Dean and I ambled on, the magenta sunset dripping over the picturesque village and expansive lake, we spent time people-watching. Here, there were no rules, just the endless, emotional chatter of haggling for goods in a ritual that many Americans loathe. I, on the other hand, love to barter. In New York or Atlanta, some government bureaucrat would probably show up wanting to see everybody's licenses and inquire if all the merchandise had passed muster with some federal agency. Or more to the point, had all these transactions been reported to the IRS?

The closest I come to this art form back home is buying tickets to a college football game from some fan or scalper. But there the capitalists are usually inebriated, their calculating and reasoning skills, if any, diminished.

I finally made the mistake of nodding to one of the young girls of almost pure Mayan blood who carried five or six colorful scarfs. She and another young girl soon assaulted us, walking down the street with us, brandishing dozens of garments. The last thing I'll ever need, or wear, is a scarf, but the young girls were so persistent, so adamant, so loveable, that I finally paused to look over one of the scarves. "*¿Cuánto cuesta para este?*"

The girl smiled. "Five American, forty Guatemalan."

"Five?" I said in English and with a smile. "*¿Usted esta loca?*"

The girl grinned. "Okay, okay. Three American dollars."

I passed off my best Spanish translation of, "How about five dollars for two, one from each of you?"

The two girls rolled their eyes, apparently not sure if they should take the offer before I changed my mind, or try to sucker me for more money.

Seeing their dismay, I pulled out a wad of Guatemalan quetzals and paid them each their initial asking price. Their smiles made my day.

The transaction only brought on five or six more of the business ladies, now strolling along beside us. I tried to wave them away. "*No más dinero.*"

One of the older ladies very persistently pursued me, babbling away in Spanish. My translation: "How come you only buy from young, pretty girls? Buy one from an old woman who works hard."

"Tough luck," I said. "Welcome to reality. Young girls have been outselling old ladies since Adam and Eve."

"What?" she mumbled.

I laughed, and she produced a big grin. This was too much for my heart and after spending a few minutes scanning the scarves and joshing her about her sewing skills, I bought another, bright turquoise scarf without even bartering. I then shooed the other women away before I had to find a bank machine just to get a taxi back to the hotel.

I put the three scarves around my neck, wondering what I would do with them. If I had a girlfriend, I could possibly give one to her, telling her that I was thinking of her way down in Guatemala. I decided to just leave the local clothing in the hotel room and possibly some other pushover would be negotiating right here in a few days for the same scarf. All in all, the haggling with the feisty Mayan women and their big friendly eyes was more than worth the fifteen dollars.

As I finally walked off double time, one of the women yelled at me, "You come see me tomorrow. My name is Margarita."

Tomorrow, I would hopefully be another two hundred miles down the road.

Guatemalans' Hospitality and Short Memory

I wanted to depart at first light the next morning, but Rafael Ralón, the hotel owner, wanted to take some pictures with us and the car. I'm quite familiar with the Latin concept of time, so about seven, I called him to make sure he was on his way.

He assured me he was en route.

To pass the time, Dean and I took a fantastic picture of us and the car on the banks of Lake Atitlán and then ate a light breakfast at the hotel. The lake may be the most beautiful natural wonder I've ever seen, a huge, volcanic caldera lake, similar in setting to Yellowstone Lake, a vast expanse of calm, shimmering water set between towering, peaceful peaks. It's ringed with three enormous, cone-shaped volcanoes: Atitlán, San Pedro, and Toliman. They reach for the sky, piercing the clouds and give eloquent testament to the powerful forces below.

I tried to pay for the car wash, but was told it was complimentary. Further ingratiating us with the hotel staff, the night before, Dean ran off a couple of American hippies, whiffing pot and walking around the hotel grounds and lakefront, setting off fireworks.

I don't know what he did, but after he set off to quiet the little heathens, the loud, irritating pops ceased.

• • •

How friendly and helpful the Guatemalans had been. Few people in the world should be more hostile to Americans than Guatemalans. They'd been the recipient of more underhanded misdealing by us over the last hundred years than almost any country on the planet. In fact, Guatemala hasn't had much luck since the Europeans arrived.

First conquered by the tyrannical Spanish conquistador Pedro de Alvarado almost five hundred years ago, it is estimated that through disease, murder, or deportation for slavery, a third of the Guatemalan population was eliminated during the first hundred years of occupation.

Later came the Americans. First, the New Orleans-based United Fruit Company and its president, Samuel Zemurray, nicknamed Sam the Banana Man, that controlled the country for most of the first half the twentieth century with monopolies not only on land and bananas, but also coffee, the postal service, railroads, and the media, just to name a few.

By 1952, the Guatemalans had had enough and elected a liberal president who planned to reform the country and end foreign exploitation. The only problem was he was too left-leaning, and Washington feared the republic might end up a puppet state for the Soviets. So in one of America's first attempts at nation building, the CIA orchestrated a coup that deposed the elected president and installed a general with more capitalistic values. Not our finest hour.

What followed was forty years of military rule and a thirty-year civil war that resulted in the death or disappearance of more than two hundred thousand Guatemalans. On a proportional basis, that's about three times as many deaths as America suffered in World War II. The United Nations estimates that government forces or CIA-trained paramilitaries were responsible for more than 90 percent of the murders. I'm glad we finally defeated those Soviets, but we had to sell our souls to do it.

Since the demise of world communism, true democracy has returned to Guatemala, and in 1996 peace accords were signed between the government and the guerrillas. Still, the healing process has been slow. In 1998, two days after his publication of *Never Again in Guatemala*, Bishop Juan José Gerardi Conedera, a long-time advocate for Guatemala's indigenous people, was beaten to death in his church. So brutal was the murder that he was identified only by his ring. In 2001, three army officers and a priest were convicted of his murder. The case was the first time members of the military had been tried in a civilian court.

Since the Guatemalans don't seem to have America's vindictiveness, and appear more worried about their future than their past, I anxiously waited on Rafael in hopes he might give me some driving directions. Not sure of our next destination or the route, I had walked down to the Hotel Atitlán the night before, hoping to find the American owners.

I didn't find them, but I did find a hotel full of well-to-do Americans, mostly middle- or late-aged couples, private-school types, dining in the plush accommodations in a scene that resembled the restaurant and bar at Washington, DC's Four Seasons. A wedding party was even at the hotel. All gave the impression of fun, schmoozing in their casual wear as they lifted wine glasses in toasts. Let's hope the marriage turns out better than most of the weddings I've been in.

The hotel clerk did speak excellent English and scratched out a few directions on my map.

Rafael finally arrived about seven-thirty with a request—he wanted us to bring the car to his other hotel in town. We could have breakfast there, and he wanted to take some pictures of the car there with his family.

I concurred, but first wanted to get some better directions. I pulled out my Central American map and unfolded it on the hood of the car. "Rafael, we're headed south, two hundred to two hundred fifty miles. Where do you think we can get a charge, and how do we get there?"

Rafael studied the map, scratching his chin, then pointed to La Libertad, El Salvador. "This is good place, plenty of hotels. And take this road." He pointed to CA-2 along the coast.

"How's the border crossing there?"

"No problem, about an hour."

I ran my hands through my hair and flashed my eyes at Dean. I knew La Libertad, a popular coastal resort with American surfers I'd briefly passed through a decade previously, but his recommended route was in complete contrast to the instructions I'd gotten the previous evening.

"How about this road, further inland?" I said, pointing at CA-1, "and then crossing here?"

Rafael crinkled his face. "That's okay too, but you will have to go through Guatemala City. Just don't take this road here." He pointed to a road that ran south out of Lake Atitlán to the coast. "Or this northern road. It has some trouble spots, and I hear the border crossing there can be problematic."

I was more confused than before. I stared at Rafael. I had long ago learned to be leery of directions meted out south of the border.

They'd sent me on dozens of goose-chases over the years. There's something in the Latin psyche, *machismo* as it's called, that makes a man embarrassed if he doesn't know the way. When in doubt, he will simply make up the directions.

But worse, our GPS that had performed superbly in Mexico had started to get befuddled since we had crossed the Mexican border. The standard Garmin package for North America includes Mexico, but Garmin doesn't produce a GPS map file for Central America. I'd been forced to purchase a third-party package. Thus far, it had done a pretty good job of mapping our location and travel direction in the mountain forest, but with directions and roads, it had been somewhat spotty. Surely, some computer whiz kid out there should put something more reliable on the market, but the number of individuals needing this would be minuscule. How many dumbasses like us are out there?

Dean spoke up. "We'll just keep the sun to our left in the mornings, and to our right in the evenings. The terrain will eventually taper us in the right direction. Just keep going south. We'll get there."

I looked at the map, the distance between the two oceans growing narrower by the day. In Guatemala, only about 225 miles separated the Pacific and Atlantic, and by the time we got to Panama, if we made it that far, this would be reduced to about forty miles. We were down to reading the map and traveling by celestial "dead reckoning!" At least we had a map.

• • •

By eight-thirty we had pacified Rafael and were on the road, our tank full. The 3,000-foot climb out of Panajachel would likely consume 10 to 15 percent of our batteries, but I wasn't concerned.

We'd be at an elevation above 8,000 feet and on our way to the coast, where the elevation was no more than 1,500 feet. In an electric car, like an airplane, elevation is stored energy, and our net descent would add considerably to our range. To my contentment, the day before, and even earlier in Mexico, the Tesla had grossly exceeded my expectations in the mountains.

Behind the wheel, I felt cautiously optimistic and again overtaken with the task ahead. We'd make it somewhere today, but the next twelve hours promised to be a true day of discovery. At our recent rates of travel, we'd be lucky to burn all our battery in twelve to fifteen hours. The long hours of getting the car down the road in recent days had left me little time to muse over my holiday. This vacation was turning out to be a lot of work, but what a great break from the world.

Climbing out of Panajachel, I got a final look at Lake Atitlán. The sun, rising in the east, shone on the land, accentuating the montage of colors and the mammoth wedge of water, stretching across the horizon and juxtaposed against the resplendent volcanoes, their chiseled apexes colliding with the sky.

• • •

Like many people living around natural wonders, the residents here had paid a price. During the civil war, Mayan villages around the lake were constantly harassed by the government. It is believed that more than three hundred citizens in the area, and Stanley Rother, a missionary from Oklahoma, were killed by government forces.

Weather has also been a source of trouble. In 2005, Hurricane Stan belted the region, inducing a huge landslide that buried the lakeside village of Panabaj, killing 1,400 and leaving 5,000 homeless. Tropical storms are forever causing rapid water-level increases on the lake, flooding the adjacent villages. Since Hurricane Stan, most of the roads had been rebuilt, and the region looked to be bouncing back fine.

But the biggest long-term threat to the lake is an environmental tragedy. Too much sewage was being discharged to the lake from the dozen or so villages around it. The tourists in Panajachel had to be making this worse. A few years ago, the lake turned green because of the oxygen-depleting effluent. Swimming is not recommended. The sewage problem is much worse than most lakes or rivers that get contaminated because the lake has no river feeding it or a natural outlet. The water is only rainfall that has collected for thousands of years, so Mother Nature provides no flushing effect to help cleanse the lake.

When a closed system like this gets polluted, it is very difficult to clean it up. Several international groups have donated more than a million dollars to address the problem, but currently the lake's situation has not improved significantly. And this in one of the most breathtaking, spectacular locales in the world.

• • •

Less than an hour outside of Panajachel, we had to make a decision. As we approached the turnoff to the road Rafael recommended, we opted to stay on CA-1. It was still a four-lane highway. Curvy and steep, the road wasn't I-10, or even anything a good-government state like Texas would be proud of (in Louisiana we'd have been damn proud of it), and I had averaged almost 40 mph for the last half hour—warp speed compared to the day before. The side road didn't look too inviting, only two lanes of asphalt disappearing into the emerald mountains. Hopefully we weren't being tempted into a trap.

Our route along CA-1 (Central American Highway 1), led right through the middle of Guatemala City, the largest city in Central America, with more than four million people in the urban area. The traffic was terrible on the six- and eight-lane route through town. On the freeway, Lexuses and Mercedes battled with 1980s hand-me-down jalopies from the States. They all jammed their way onto and off the road with little order. In the mayhem, they dodged and cut everywhere. The drivers honked as if this were required to prime the engine.

Nothing worried me more than the thought of a crash. Each day, fewer obstacles lay in front of us, but with each day we had more to lose in a mishap.

Our biggest impediment were the lunatic drivers. For the natives, driving, and more importantly passing, is a race, something to be relished. At home, most Americans cautiously slow down and ease over when changing lanes in a traffic jam, giving other drivers time to yield and make way. Here, they storm into the other lane, hoping to beat everybody else to the desired spot.

I can think of no better use for American foreign aid than giving defensive-driving lessons to the entire third world. And probably nothing would increase the average human's life span more.

The urban driving was the most frightening, for here we had the best chance for a fender-bender too complicated for the local body shop. While the open road wasn't any safer—the drivers equally incompetent—the odds there were more in our favor. Of course, on the open road, the stakes are higher—the loss of the car or the trip might be a minor inconvenience compared with the consequences of meeting one of these nutcases at 70 mph.

Four times during our transit of Guatemala City we were funneled off the road and into a neighborhood. It wasn't like we were driving in the exit lane—suddenly, the middle of the road would split, three lanes going one way and three lanes going the other. The signs on the freeway would say something like: *Calle 20 to the right, Avenida 14 to the left.* Nothing said how to stay on CA-1. There may be something to that sign-selling enterprise I mentioned a few chapters back. I thought to check into that when I got home. It had to be less stressful than engineering.

Every time we found ourselves off the freeway, we were forced to drive around the neighborhood for a few blocks until we got back on the freeway. Fortunately, we were never dumped off into the Guatemalan version of East LA. After our first two wrong turns, I approached these devious splits with intense focus in hopes of finding something to steer me correctly. A few times I guessed right. The GPS was of no use. As I agonized over what to do at each moment of truth, all it said was, "Calculating."

After forty-five minutes of the nerve-racking experience, we found ourselves out of town, having seen none of the shantytowns, or "settlements," the city is notorious for. Or felt the danger I'd heard so much about. Fifteen or twenty miles south of Guatemala City, the road transitioned back to a congested two-lane, winding, pothole-strewn asphalt trail bisecting the rural landscape. Despite the good road out of Panajachel, it had taken us almost four hours to go 120 miles, and our pace was about to slow down. Outside, the scenery hadn't changed: green hills, impoverished villages, and pickup trucks, their beds crammed with people.

We drove by Volcano Pacaya, its sharp apex only nine miles off to our right. A month later, it would erupt, sending a vertical stream of ash, gas, and glowing rock two and a half miles high.

We did find a couple of short stretches where we were vectored off the old road onto new four-lane that took a straight line, the engineers carving away the hills for the new throughway. Just as our hopes rose on one of these, we'd be back on the old road. But the signs of progress were encouraging. Maybe they could get the highway completed before the radical environmentalists found out about it and started complaining about spoiling the virgin country.

We passed four or five more volcanoes. Our only sight in this stretch of road was the crossing of the often-raging *Rio los Esclavos*, the River of Slaves, at the little town of Cuilapa. We passed just beside the old stone bridge, built by the Spanish in 1592 and still in operation. Only recently has motorized traffic been removed from the bridge, not because of structural deficiency, but in hopes of prolonging the lifespan of the engineering treasure.

At a fork, we took CA-8 to avoid the road Rafael had warned us about. From here, it was about thirty miles to the El Salvador border.

· · ·

I'd noticed that, as we approached borders, the land became isolated, and this stretch of road was the most solitary we'd driven the entire trip. We saw nothing but a few women carrying wood on their heads. Americans often forget how good we have it.

In an exceptionally bad mood, Dean didn't say much during the day. His computer had crashed the night before. His daily video posts had come to an end, as had his work on a website for the trip that he had been putting together in both English and Chinese.

"When we get to the next town," I said, "just go buy a new one."

"I don't roll like you and all your highfalutin' buddies," he jested, "who think everything you have is disposable—clothes, computers, even cars. When the shit quits working, you just trash it and flop down your credit card for a new one. When you live in some of the overseas places I do, you gotta know how to fix or salvage everything."

I looked at the GPS. It was doing a reasonable job of tracking our progress. The little border town of Valle Nuevo was only a few miles ahead. I looked back out at Guatemala. It had been an enjoyable surprise, its land superlative, its people polite and helpful. Grave predictions abound from narco experts and pundits that Guatemala is on the verge of becoming the next Mexico. Let's hope not. I'd like to come back some day. Hopefully, El Salvador would be as agreeable.

Guatemalan Math
and Bridges

The first thing that tells you that you're at a Central American border crossing is not the signs, or the customs or immigration buildings, but the hawkers, helpers, handlers, shysters, petty con men, you name it, who loiter around the border crossings hoping to prey on unsuspecting tourists. They attack you like hornets who have just had their nest kicked.

When we drove up to the tiny Guatemalan border crossing in Valle Nuevo in the freshly washed, slick new Tesla, they recklessly charged forward. Dogs will run at a car, but they have enough sense to chase behind the car when they get close. Not these people. They ran directly in front.

"What the hell?" I slammed on the brakes.

Three or four heads poked into my window, forcing me to roll it up as I motored up to a small, official-looking building.

"*No necesito*," I said four or five times as I stepped out of the car, grabbing my papers and locking the door.

My words dissuaded no one, and the hawkers continued to blare Spanish into my face, a few less than a foot away. One man grabbed my arm and another reached for my passport and papers.

We braved the crowd and uncomfortable setting, managing to enter the little building where we had our passports stamped. I was then told to go to customs next door. This went rather quickly, but the agent wanted copies of my registration and passport that I didn't have.

One of the hawkers who had followed me inside barked in my ear, "I make copies, two dollars, American only."

I looked at the little man, trying to size him up, then at the customs agent who nodded. I removed my wallet and pulled out twenty dollars, all that I had, and handed it to the man.

"Just a minute," he said and ran off.

Patiently waiting, I decided to change the Guatemalan quetzals in my wallet for some dollars, the official currency of El Salvador. I approached one of the money changers and handed him eight hundred quetzals.

I've spent a lot of my life in gutters, but the little con man had perfected one of the most ingenious scams I'd ever seen. He quickly pulled out his calculator, held it up in front of me and divided 800 by 7.7, the current exchange rate. The calculator screen produced 27.6. The little outlaw raised up his wad of cash, counted out the twenty-seven dollars, and handed it and some change to me.

I looked at the money, my mind racing. Something wasn't right. Eight hundred quetzals should be about a hundred American dollars. I complained and asked him to redo the calculation. He raised the calculator up again, showing it to me and three other hawkers now standing around and watching. This time I took special care to watch him key the numbers and function buttons, but again the screen produced 27.6.

Perplexed, I wondered if American math and Guatemalan math were different sciences. I finally figured it out. The little thief had obviously switched the buttons on the calculator. The divide button was now something else, some exponential or maybe a pro-gramed function that produced a value smaller than the proper exchange value. How many tourists, or undereducated Americans, had he pulled this trick on? My first college degree was in math-ematics, so I'm officially a math whiz. I asked to see the calculator. He protested, only dividing the numbers again to show me all was correct.

My anger rising, there wasn't much I could do. He had my 800 quetzals and the entire crowd agreed with his little machine. The man who took my title and registration arrived with the copies, but no change.

"*Me cambio,*" I said.

The man only shrugged. "*Un momento.*"

I grabbed the copies, gave them to the customs agent, and spent another ten minutes signing papers before I got my sign-off. I looked back over my shoulder. The copy man had disappeared.

Dean sat in the passenger seat, the door locked and the win-dows rolled up.

"Let's get the hell out of here," I said.

I drove on, through the two-mile neutral zone, hoping the El Salvador border wouldn't be as big a mess. In only a few minutes, we approached the bridge over the Rio Paz. The only problem, the bridge was closed, a big crane parked on its deck.

"What now?" I moaned, pulling up to the bridge.

Four or five cars and a dozen people mingled around the bridge. I parked and stepped out. Three policemen stood beside their car.

"*¿A que hora vamos el puente?*" I said.

"Three-thirty," one of the men politely answered.

My watch read one-thirty. I'm very familiar with bridges rul-ing my life, and the complexities these pose when not functioning.

We Louisianans live with the ever-consuming challenge of having our freedoms dictated by them. They're everywhere, and you typically can't go anywhere without finding a bridge to get you there. Hopefully this wouldn't be a major ordeal.

Dean and I went over our options. We had about 120 miles of range in the car, but we had passed nothing since Guatemala City, 70 miles behind us. To get to the other border crossings in the area would take a couple of hours of valuable daylight and critical range for the car. If we waited here and got across the bridge, we'd still have to clear customs and immigrations. No telling what that would entail. It might be close to five before we got moving again, and all this depended on the bridge actually opening at three-thirty.

We'd only have an hour and a half of daylight to find some civilization and a charge. I pulled out our map and only guidebook, *Lonely Planet's Central America on a Shoestring*, 2013.

There were two towns across the border: Ahuachapán, population 38,000 and ten miles across the Rio Paz, and Sonsonate, population 65,000 and thirty miles across the border. *Lonely Planet* mentioned that Sonsonate was home to some of El Salvador's most notorious gangs. Applying my correction of a Central American city's population to the possible services, finding ample lodging, and charging would be difficult, especially late in the day or after dark.

But I had a bigger concern. In Latin America, three-thirty can often mean five, or even three-thirty the next day. On the Guatemalan side of the border, only four or five derelict shacks were built into the side of the two steep hills on each side of the road. The cars now backed up past a curve, as far as I could see.

A second, more immediate problem loomed. My gut stirred. I needed to find a restroom. There was nothing at the border crossing, and the hills beside the road were too steep to use the portable potty. I scouted the situation.

Dean had gotten friendly with the three Guatemalan guards. He now had the hood open and the guards were taking pictures of each other with the car.

I explained my situation to one of the guards and he told me there was a bathroom on the other side of the bridge. I could walk across to El Salvador and potty. Perfect. I'd solve my problem, clear my mind, and as I cantered over the bridge, the civil engineer in me would review the repair issue and make an educated guess as to if or when we'd get to cross.

The stomach problem only cost a quarter to fix, and on my way back, my inspection of the bridge told me the work wouldn't be finished for weeks. The crew was pulling rebar to replace the concrete deck. The bridge closing was obviously only a scheduled daily closing for the work. No critical part had to be repaired or replaced to open it. The workers simply had to stop work and open the bridge.

I spent a few minutes examining the exquisite suspension bridge, a fine work of art and engineering. I later discovered that the structure was somewhat of a forgotten jewel. It hadn't been painted in decades, but looked fine, sturdy. Completed in 1949 by John A. Roebling and Sons, the builders of the Brooklyn Bridge, it was designed by Charles Sutherland, Roebling's chief engineer on the George Washington Bridge in New York City. The bridge had a 209-foot main span and employed some of the first pre-stressing technology in bridge building. If this place was in the middle of nowhere now, I could only imagine how remote it must have been then.

Nonetheless, sixty-five years later, the twenty-first-century engineering marvel was waiting on the twentieth-century marvel to be patched up with nineteenth-century techniques.

Back at the car, I picked up the map again. There was the option of driving down to the coast, only forty miles away. It shortened the distance to La Libertad to only seventy-five miles.

The night before, I'd done a little internet research on one of the coastal towns near the border. There was little, but one traveler had posted something to the order of: "Great waves. Recommend day trip only. If you do stay, don't travel at night and secure your car and belongings." So it went when overlanding in Central America.

I asked the guards about the coast road to La Libertad. Maybe the coast had other tourist towns, but I was quickly told the road was bad and passed through no towns of significance. As I continued to look for an impossible solution, I heard Dean conversing with someone in fluent English.

I got out of the car and introduced myself to Mario Aviles, a healthy, five-foot-four-inch, black-headed, fair-skinned El Salvadoran with a wife and kids in Dallas who earned his living importing and exporting. He had gotten to the bridge by driving his BMW motorcycle around the line of cars. We showed Mario the car, which he appreciated. Wanting his advice, I told him our problem and asked if he knew a good spot for us to sleep and charge.

With a big smile, he said, "No problem. I'll just lead you guys to San Salvador. It's about sixty miles. I know a short cut. I also have a friend at the Marriot Courtyard. He'll get you a charge. I'll call him to see if it's okay."

I studied Mario. This was too good to be true. Could he be our savior? He didn't look or sound like the immoral type. "We don't drive very fast. It drains our batteries."

"No problem. I'll call my friend now."

"Many thanks," I said, hoping our problem might be solved.

• • •

At about three, the construction crew began to wrap up, and the bridge scene transitioned from despair to optimism. I looked across

the Rio Paz to El Salvador. We'd be in our third country sometime today, hopefully. What an adventure. Studying the scraggly,
brush-covered brown hills, I couldn't help but wonder if we were
being lowered into a fiery caldron or deadly crevasse where return,
at least with the car, would be unlikely.

In no time, we rolled over Mr. Sutherland's masterpiece and
were routed to the right side of the far bank by a border guard. I got
out with all my papers. Through the unruly scene, I conversed with
one of the agents as a mangy dog tried to make love to my leg. The
agent needed copies and pointed to a little store. The proprietor
was honest and provided the service for two dollars.

After fifteen minutes of turmoil, we were ordered to the other
side of the road. There we parked and went inside to present our
papers.

A polite El Salvadoran soon inspected the car, but then the
problems started. What they were, I didn't know. I sat on a bench,
smoking cigarettes as the minutes passed, by the tens.

Mario had pulled his motorcycle up and continued to patiently
wait, conversing with Dean. Finally, after forty-five minutes, I asked
Mario if he could lend a hand.

He gladly agreed and entered the building. A few minutes
later he returned to explain the problem. The international customs
declaration forms for vehicles require both a VIN number and an
engine number. The problem: the Tesla didn't have an engine, which
perplexed the bureaucrats—how to fill in all the blanks? I would
later learn, much to my chagrin, this was not a problem unique to
El Salvadoran customs agents.

I considered bribery, but another man approached, an older,
educated-looking Salvadoran who spoke English. He began to
chew some ass, lambasting the officials. My guess at the translation: "These are tourists, just wanting to come visit our country.

You wonder why the world thinks we're a banana republic? Yada, yada . . ."

I sat down on the bench and lit up. We'd been across the bridge more than an hour and a half. It was after five, the shadows growing long. I couldn't believe that Mario still patiently and politely waited for us.

Ten more minutes passed, our problems besieging me. Where would we stay tonight? I walked over to Mario, feeling guilty that he'd waited so long. "I don't know if they'll let us go or not. You don't have to wait on us."

Mario picked up our map, circling the best route, and writing his phone number on it. "I'll wait a little longer, but here are the directions, and my number. Just call me when you get close to San Salvador."

I spied the sun, hanging over the horizon. San Salvador seemed like a reach.

One of the customs agents emerged from the building, handing me some paperwork.

"I can go?" I said in Spanish.

"*Sí.*" The man nodded.

Not believing my ears, I pointed. "San Salvador?"

Smiling, the man nodded again. "*Sí, sí.* No more."

Our ordeal had ended. The only good news was that again the paperwork had been too cumbersome for Dean to get a driving permit. I turned to Mario. "How about you just lead us there? Don't worry about the speed. I'll keep up."

In the waning daylight, we followed Mario (driving more like Evel Knievel) and his BMW that raced around curves and volcanoes, passed cars, switched lanes, and made several turns. Possibly, the writer from *Frommer's* had been following Mario on one of his excursions through Central America when he wrote that passage about the driving in Guatemala.

One of the volcanoes we passed was the massive Izalco, an ominous, intimidating pyramid of gray rock and cinder blotting the horizon. It was once active enough to earn the title, "Lighthouse of the Pacific."

"Mario told me," Dean said, "that El Salvador doesn't have any *topes*."

Too busy to look up, I replied, "The roads are a hell of lot better than Guatemala, that's for sure."

Dean lifted up our guidebook. "*Lonely Planet* says there are half-a-million guns in El Salvador. It's a gun toting society."

"How many people in El Salvador?"

"Six million."

"We've only got four-and-a-half million people in Louisiana, and I bet we've got ten million guns. I'll take guns over *topes* any day."

At twilight, Mario led us into San Salvador, through a dizzying maze of roads, freeways, turns, interchanges, and on and off ramps. I didn't know if we were going east or west, and neither did the GPS. Soon, we took two rapid turns, went through a large traffic circle, and out of nowhere, pulled up at the seven-story Courtyard beside a modern pedestrian mall.

Mario pulled off his helmet, shaking out his thick black hair. He walked into the hotel and soon appeared with his friend, César. Hotel guests and staff came to look over the car with the now typical Latin awe.

César smiled as Mario hopped back on the BMW and rode off. He then led us around to the back of the hotel. In the mechanical room, beside three big boilers, he showed me a socket, a modern three-pole, 240-volt, 30-amp outlet.

In Spanish, César conveyed only one request before we were allowed to hook up to the lifeline—he and a few of the staff wanted to look at the car and get some pictures. I patiently waited as the Salvadorans crawled in and out of the car, snapping pictures, their friendly smiles stretching ear to ear.

I too produced a big grin as I pulled out our charging adapter. In only an hour and half, we'd gone from a hopeless situation, our worst of the trip, to the best setup since McAllen.

We Ain't in Orange County

I'd been to San Salvador once, seven or eight years before. It's rumored to have the best nightlife in Central America so I hoped we might finally get in some late-night entertainment. As I checked in to the hotel, I asked the cute girl at the hotel's front desk for an after-hours recommendation.

She cocked her head back, exposing her long, smooth black locks and wonderful bronze skin, before flashing her deep brown eyes to Dean and then me. "The national elections are tomorrow. The law mandates no alcohol is sold in the country for three days before the election." She smiled. "Sorry."

"Not anywhere?" I asked.

"No."

Dean spoke up. "That's some crazy shit . . . voting with a clear conscience and without chemical enhancement? These Central Americans are getting serious about this democracy."

I chuckled. "In Louisiana, elected officials would be tarred and feathered for this."

The young girl looked at me with perplexed eyes.

"It's a gringo joke," I said, returning her smile and walking off.

El Salvador's election laws may have been a blessing, because our charging situation wasn't as ideal as I'd initially thought. Though

I'd set the charging rate at 26 amps, we'd flipped the 30-amp breaker after only two hours of charging. This was the third time this had happened since leaving the States, further mystifying my simple little brain when it came to determining available power. Luckily, I realized it by nine, while César was still at work, and he had the hotel maintenance man reset the fuse. Checking the car's trip meter, we'd gone 234 miles that day in ten grueling hours. I set the charge rate at 17 amps and did a quick calculation. We'd be fully charged by ten-thirty the next morning.

I then walked next door to the pedestrian mall to buy a large cheese pizza from Pizza Hut. Heading back to our room, I picked up a recent copy of *The New York Times* that somebody had discarded in the hotel lobby and skimmed the headlines. Not much going on in the States, just the everyday stories—the Republicans and Democrats fighting about everything, something about the drought in California, and a story about the Super Bowl, to be played the next day.

Back home I devour the news, reading three or four local papers daily, and any number of national news websites. The *Times* didn't pique my interest. I had all but divested myself from the twenty-four-hour news cycle that saturates daily life in America. It didn't really seem that relevant now. Mine was a simple existence, my only purpose: finding 240-volt electrical sockets, daily sustenance, a roof over my head, avoiding bandits, and not getting lost. My only guide was the compass.

I spent an hour sending Marcus some more pictures of the car at the border crossings and Lake Atitlán. He had the day before called Dean complaining that we needed to send him more pictures with the car in front of famous places or signs.

"We ain't in Orange County, where you can drive out to Disneyland and take a picture with Mickey Mouse," Dean reminded him. "We're in the jungle. Nothing to see, maybe some cows and huts. And if that car's not moving, it's charging. It takes every hour of daylight to get it down the road and plugged up."

Munching on the pizza and drinking a Coke, I tried to do some planning for the next day. I had no idea where we were headed or how we'd get there. The first chore was to find out where we were in San Salvador, a city of more than a million and a half. Google Maps found the Courtyard. We were fortunate. The hotel was only a mile away from the Pan American Highway. The bad news: we had barely gotten into San Salvador and had to cross almost all of the metropolis the next day. Hopefully the signs would be clearer here than they were in Guatemala City—though I didn't hold out much hope.

I spent thirty minutes painstakingly writing out directions to get us out of town. The problem was: *where* to go? Studying the map, I settled on Choluteca, Honduras, 187 miles away, but on CA-1. Our *Lonely Planet* had only three paragraphs about Choluteca, stating it was an agricultural center with banks and gas stations. It mentioned no hotels. Wikipedia said it had about one hundred thousand residents. One site said that year-round it may be the hottest place on the planet. That was more bad news as the Tesla's power-consuming AC was off limits for us. Tripadvisor.com listed only one hotel.

My pizza lost its flavor. We had few if any options in case something happened and we had to stop short. There was nothing past Choluteca for eighty miles, and worse, nothing before it for ninety miles. El Salvador is only about the size of Massachusetts, but we had to navigate the country's long axis. Worse, east El Salvador is known as the "Wild East," a guerrilla stronghold during the country's thirteen-year civil war that ended in 1992.

• • •

In that bloody affair, seventy-five thousand people met their maker, proportionally similar to America's losses in World War II. Some of the worst atrocities were in the northern portion of the State of San Vicente, which we'd be driving right across. The most notable of these was the 1982 El Calabozo Massacre of more than two hundred, including children. And yes, the perpetrators were the notorious Atlacatl Battalion of the Salvadoran Army, trained and backed by the United States.

Keeping those communists at bay was dirty work for sure. Of course, the revolutionaries didn't help their cause much. The current ruling party took its name from the guerrilla army, FMLN (Farabundo Martí National Liberation Front), named after one of the founders of the Communist Party of Central America. Maybe Central American leftists should take some cues from the Americans who have mastered deception and spin. You kiss and tickle the baby when stealing his lollipop, not pinch him.

El Salvador has put much of its past behind it. Its problem today is not guerrillas or government death squads, but gangs, called *maras.* These are more like conventional American-style outlaws, interested in everyday crimes—drugs, extortion, theft, turf wars. In fact, most were founded in big American cities after more than a million Salvadorans fled to the States during the civil war. We exported them back home, our government deciding it was cheaper to deport than imprison them. Security has become a booming business in El Salvador, with eighteen thousand security guards. The government forces that once hunted left-wing revolutionaries now hunt the *maras,* but with a new, sinister name: *Sombra Negra,* Black Shadow.

The *maras* are so powerful that in 2009 they shut down the country's entire bus system. To protest proposed anti-gang laws, they put out the word—any bus driver working would "face the consequences." The gangs agreed to a cease-fire in 2012, but the recent discovery of some mass graves might indicate the *maras* are still not behaving as model citizens.

Did I mention the country is rocked by perpetual earthquakes? San Salvador is destroyed about once a century. Fortunately for us, the last gigantic tremor had been only twenty-seven years earlier, when 1,500 died and more than a 100,000 lost their homes.

• • •

I studied the map for clues. Central American maps aren't like Rand McNally maps of Florida. Red lines run all over them, but by this time I well knew that just because the map has a red line, even a bold red line, doesn't mean a highway. It might mean a gravel washout or grass trail.

We had fewer options than at any time on the trip thus far. A misstep on the way to Choluteca had the possibility for consequences—real consequences. Our options were minimal, likely in the most rural and dangerous place we'd be in the seven countries, with no civilization for several hours' drive in any direction.

• • •

I love maps. My house and office are full of framed atlases and maps, which is probably one of the reasons I became an engineer and surveyor. In another century, maybe I'd have been one of the intrepid men who mapped the world. I like to think so anyway.

What a true adventure of discovery those must have been. Unfortunately for my generation, there are no more places left to discover, no more regions to map. Still, I've always enjoyed identifying canyons or mountains on a map, or the simple pleasure of finding my way across an unknown country with only a topographic chart to guide me.

But this was the real thing—1,900 miles from the nearest first-world, English-speaking country, in a car that only goes 265 miles a day. Did I already mention that Honduras is the murder capital of the world? Well, El Salvador is number two. For both countries, these murder rates are more than three times higher than Mexico, where crime draws the world's attention. It's best to move through these areas quickly, with a low profile. In a dashing new Tesla, you'd just as well paint a target on you.

This troubled a part of me. I thought I was born for this type of stuff, using my wits to traverse difficult places. But now, at the precipice, my plain life back in the States didn't seem so uninviting.

My fingers moved across the keyboard. The USGS has a wonderful new site, www.earthexplorer.com. The terrain feature on it makes Google Earth seem like something for kindergarteners. The page has incredible detail, allowing the user to zoom in and read twenty-meter contours and the names of small streams and roads.

I'd be here for the next few hours, glued to the computer screen.

• • •

The next morning I took advantage of the hotel's hospitality, having two copies made of all the car's paperwork. I didn't want to be hustled by another dishonest copy man. As I patiently waited for the copies, taking breakfast at the hotel, I met a woman from

Indiana. Her daughter had married a Salvadoran, and though they all now lived in Indiana, he'd returned to El Salvador to work on the election. She'd tagged along to look after her granddaughter during the campaign.

Dean and I planned to depart at nine, with our batteries only 90 percent charged. This was a first for the trip, unplugging from reliable 240-volt power without being fully charged, especially in such a secure location. But we had a border to cross, and we'd learned our lesson the day before about teasing twilight. Not to mention that the Super Bowl kicked off at five-thirty.

My hand-written directions worked. We made it out of San Salvador with only a single wrong turn, and that one only minor.

At a red light, American gangsta-rap music spilled out on the street from the car beside us. Over the F-bombs and other adjectives, I wondered if the passengers understood the words, or just enjoyed the thumping, rhythmic beat. Was this the real gangster paradise?

The roads were good, four-lane until we got about thirty miles outside the capital. There, they tapered back to two-lane. Though crowded, the roads were relatively straight, and for the most part had some type of shoulder. But the Salvadoran drivers seem to have the same desire for quick death as their Guatemalan neighbors.

The potholes were abundant, but not as bad as before, most only a few inches in depth instead of feet. I highly advise investing in a new set of tires before driving in Latin America.

This was election day. Like the day before, trucks and cars of every type rolled up and down the roads, adorned with colorful flags. El Salvador is a world away from Guatemala. Less than one percent indigenous, physically its citizens display more European traits than most Central American countries. Even with income levels considerably higher than its neighbors, the country, like most in the developing world, has a highly polarized right and left. As with the rest of Central America, remittances from expatriates, mostly in the United States, still constitute a sizable portion of its GDP.

The country is still slowly emerging from its long civil war. Even the election today pitted the incumbent party's candidate, FMLN's Sánchez Cerén, a former guerrilla commander and current vice president, against the country's establishment. Somewhere along the way, the FMLN had transitioned from an armed revolutionary movement into a political party. As we motored across their former stronghold, we were glad the natives had decided to settle their differences with the ballot box instead of with guns.

Maybe the politicians here actually wanted to solve some problems. And the voters could actually choose one side or the other. Back home, we never knew what we were voting for or getting. The Democrats want to regulate everything and have the government take care of us, but they want social freedom. The Republicans want no government, but they want to tell us who we can sleep with or what we could smoke or drink. Hypocrisy is the common ground.

Anyway, while the Salvadorans decided their fate, we passed through Llopango, Cojutepeque, and San Vicente, all four hundred or five hundred years old with shady plazas, lively markets, and outlandishly colorful houses. Then over the Rio Lempa, the third-longest river in Central America. More sugarcane and rolling hills spiked with volcanoes. The fiery mountains were all starting to look the same, but one was puffing steam pretty good, which I thought was neat.

I later learned the volcano, named San Miguel, only fifteen miles outside of the city by the same name, had erupted only a month earlier, spewing ash and smoke that forced the evacuation of thousands. I guess the smoking time bomb is only neat if you're some type of fruity American scooting by as you run from your first-world midlife doldrums because your existence has gotten too cushy and mundane.

We drove on and on, through San Miguel, population about two hundred thousand, just before noon. There are no bypasses when traveling in Latin America. We puttered down Main Street after Main Street on our traverse of the eastern branch of the Pacific Ring of Fire, bumping along at 5 or 10 mph, dodging everything imaginable. San Miguel was no different. Horns honked. Citizens and cars jockeyed for the road, swearing or gesturing rudely at each other. As we paused for a herd of goats, we saw a gentleman with the worst job in Central America—the pedestrian traffic cop trying to sort it all out.

Outside of town, we entered a complicated traffic circle. The GPS didn't know what to do, but lo and behold, three signs led me through with simple arrows pointing out how to stay on CA-1!

A shortcut appeared just outside San Miguel that knocked fifteen miles off our trip. The road looked good, but the street sign read "Ruta Militar." We decided to play it safe and stay on CA-1.

From here, it was forty miles to the Honduran border. The road again got lonely—nothing. We did get our first glimpse of the Pacific Ocean, at the Bay of Unión, while passing through a few small, dirty towns.

The biggest eyesore on Central American roads is the abundant trash, piled up or blowing in the wind like autumn leaves. Outside of the exclusive residential, tourist, or business districts, it's almost as abundant as grass. Possibly, this is seen by the citizens as some type of year-round accent, like holiday lighting back home. In the States, we may have an abundance of hooligans and homeless, but at least they have clean sidewalks to sleep on or ply their trades.

I didn't know how fast to drive as there were only three or four speed-limit signs in El Salvador. Somehow, we hadn't been stopped by any cops or military checkpoints. In fact, we hadn't seen many police. Maybe it was the election.

Ten miles from the border, we passed a shack with a dozen shifty-looking characters hanging around. As we passed, four or five got in a black SUV and pulled onto the road behind us.

"You see that?" I asked Dean.

"Yeah."

Constantly watching the road and my mirror, I contemplated my options. "Think I ought to step on it? There's nothing in this country that has a chance of catching this Tesla."

"Don't know." Dean turned around to get a better look.

The SUV rushed up behind us. My palms got wet, my breath short. As we wavered, the SUV raced past us. I half expected it to slow down and block the road, but they topped a hill and drove out of sight.

I lit a cigarette, scanning my mirrors and the road ahead. "That border station can't get here fast enough for me."

Randy in Chiapas, Mexico

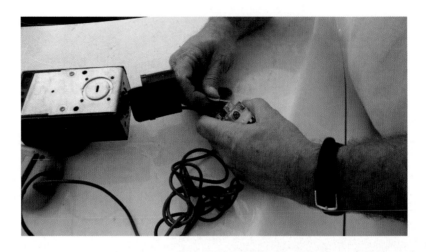

(Above) Rigging a plug in Comitan, Mexico

(Right) Panamanian electrician wiring us a plug in Penonome, Panama

(Below) Recharging in San Luis Potosi, Mexico

Dean posing with the car in Comitan, Mexico

A rural checkpoint in Panama

Dean with Guatemalan police at Rio Pas Bridge

Corrupt Honduran police

Mayan girl suckering Randy in Panajachel, Guatemala

Randy getting directions from Rafael in Guatemala

Cow in the road in Honduras

Goats at the Guatemala border

Lake Atitlán in Guatemala

Volcano in Nicaragua

Randy and Dean at the Panama Canal

Fleeced or Robbed?

We rounded a curve. The solitary road transitioned into a line of 18-wheelers, parked on the shoulder and stretching as far as the eye could see. I slammed on the brakes as the hawkers and handlers again ambushed us, madly pointing and screaming for us to pull in behind the trucks. These ruffians were more organized than the ones at the Guatemala-El Salvador border.

They had a truck that quickly pulled up, blocking us from going ahead. Red flags rushed into my head as I rolled up the windows. A police car of some type rolled down the road, forcing the villains to move the truck. I quickly pulled in behind the official car and drove forward, four or five of the hawkers jumping in the truck and following us to the El Salvador immigration office.

We managed to fight them off and get stamped out of El Salvador in only twenty minutes. Going back to the car, we were again ambushed. One of the pests who spoke a little English kept mumbling that he could help. Dean nodded something to him, and he must have interpreted this as a yes. As I opened the car door, Hector quickly hopped in the back seat.

Not sure what to do, I cautiously motored forward, over a bridge and the Río Goascorán. As we landed back on terra firma, a guard, in standard camos and armed with a M-16, stopped us.

Hector jumped out, and soon Dean and I were presenting our papers. Not drawing any positive response, I tried to show the guard the car. He was neither amused nor fascinated, never changing the iron expression on his dark face.

The guard growled several times through clenched teeth, asking us a few questions. Where were we from and why were we driving?

Fifteen minutes passed. What to do? A friend of Hector arrived, a short, thick fellow named William who spoke much better English. He started to explain. The traffic was backed up, something about the election in El Salvador, but he could fix it.

I looked around, analyzing the situation. We were the only car around. Nothing was moving. The border guard made no attempt to do anything. He had handed me my paperwork fifteen minutes earlier, and now paid us no mind, other than making it known we could not proceed.

William spoke to the guard, and then instructed us to pull forward a couple of hundred yards and wait. There, I saw no government buildings, and we got out of the car to wait in the utterly shoddy little border town. The Tesla's thermometer read 98 degrees on February 1. We took a picture with the car beside a brick structure with a big sign that said: "Welcome to Honduras."

With nothing else to do, I sat on the sidewalk, eyeing the dismal dump, one of the most unsavory places I've ever laid eyes on. We looked to be the only vehicle crossing the border, all the trucks parked and not moving. A dozen ramshackle and abandoned buildings, wood or cinder block, abutted the road around piles of discarded trash. The heat amplified the stench. Several nasty prostitutes and drug addicts solicited us for money.

Twenty or thirty minutes later William arrived, wagging his finger and explaining all kinds of problems: Election Day, there was no paperwork for an electric car, we needed to pay the officials. He said it would cost 350 dollars, and he needed 150 dollars now. I sensed fraud in his heart, but out of options, gave him 100 dollars.

He disappeared, arriving back ten minutes later. "It's 350 dollars," William said, "The permit is 50 dollars, and you have pay three officials 100 dollars each. Or you're going nowhere today. That's it. Take it or leave it."

I looked around for a government official. I saw no one, not even a building except the fumigation station a hundred yards further up the road. Dean and I complained. I finally saw someone in a uniform across the street. I tried to get his attention, but he avoided me, disappearing behind a building.

It was afternoon, and it appeared we were out of options. If 300 dollars would get us out of this situation, I was prepared to pay it. I pulled out my wallet. It had 250 dollars in it. I gave it all to William, showing him I had no more. He disappeared again.

Dean and I discussed the situation, our concern growing. We had nowhere to go. It was fifty miles back to any civilization in El Salvador, if we could even get back into the country.

"We're being robbed." I said. "The bad news is . . . It looks like these thieves are in bed with the guys with guns. We better step easy, real easy. You still got that 200 bucks hidden?"

Dean nodded.

"Give it to me." I smoked a few cigarettes, worrying.

The minutes passed. William and one of his shady sidekicks finally showed up with our paperwork, but now wanted two hundred dollars more before handing over the documents required for departure.

Concerned, Dean and I both got in the car. I didn't know what to do. Wanting to find a government official, I thought I'd ride ahead. There had to be a guard somewhere before we departed the border zone, but as I got in the car, William and his cohort jumped in the back seat, instructing us to go forward.

Alarm bells went off in my mind. My pulse quickened. Why were these hoodlums so insistent on getting in our car? Did they just want 200 more dollars for our paperwork? Clearly, they and the guards worked together. What else did they want? I don't know anybody that feels comfortable with two strangers hopping in the backseat of their car, especially in the world's most murderous country—especially if those two strangers have already fleeced you for 350 dollars. If we were asked to get out of the car and go inside somewhere, we'd be forced to the leave the car with them.

I sucked in a very deep breath and drove forward until I saw a guard at the fumigation station. I stopped, but before I had a chance to say anything, William handed the guard some money and pointed for me to drive on.

I looked at the guard, my eyes inquiring. "What do I do?" I asked in Spanish.

The guard said nothing, no expression at all, only motioning me forward and then turned around and walked off.

William pointed forward. I didn't know what to do, I wanted to just haul ass, but they were in the car, and the authorities didn't seem too interested in lending a hand. Ahead, lay open road and fifty miles of unpopulated country. Confusion besieged me as I brought the car to a stop.

"Go, go," William yelled from the back seat, his tone urgent. "And give me two hundred dollars."

I turned to look in the backseat. William continued to urge me on. My palms got wet, my heart pounded. Ahead, five or six more shady characters hovered around a shack. The tension mounted. I wanted the hooligans out of the car, now. I finally put the car in park, making sure the guard-stand behind us was still in sight.

William got adamant, pushing his head between the seats and over the center console, bitching loudly with a stern voice and serious face. He mumbled some quick Spanish I didn't understand, then snarled, "More money."

I asked to see the papers, my concern growing. William and his buddy didn't appear to be armed, at least not with guns, but they obviously had plenty of friends with them. The sons of bitches stealing the car seemed a real possibility. I half wanted to get out and give the little punks what they needed, a good Louisiana ass-whupping. Dean would be on board. In fact, for a second, I thought he was about to initiate the process.

William's crony finally presented the papers.

My patience gone, I snatched the papers. I wasn't going any further with two crooks in the car.

Dean opened the door and put a foot on the pavement.

To my surprise, William and his junior jumped out of the car, both confronting Dean, their voices growing louder.

Fear and confusion filled my spinning head. Were they about to steal the car? Everything got quick. I raised a hand, flashing our last two hundred dollars, leaned over the passenger seat and threw the money out the door, hoping one of the thugs would take it. "That's it. That's all I've got."

William looked at the money as his partner moved around to my side of the car. "How much more you got? Give it all to me." He said sternly, bending over to pick up the money.

As he did, my instinct took over. I slipped the car into drive and eased forward a few inches.

Dean ducked back in and slammed the door.

My throat thick, on the edge of my seat, I stomped on the accelerator, racing ahead. We shot by the shack and six other hooligans fifty yards in front of us. Fifteen seconds passed, my gaze roving back and forth between the road and my mirrors. We rounded a curve, putting the area out of sight. The Tesla now topped 60 mph. I saw nothing behind us, but as we rounded another sharp curve, a big cow stood in the road, a reminder of the problems with fleeing anything down here. I swerved and missed it, driving on.

Ten tense minutes passed, Dean and I both quiet, our faces red, our minds confused. We saw not a car coming or going. Finally, to my relief, we approached a military checkpoint. The stop was standard, the polite soldiers lessening my tension slightly.

Still unsettled, we drove on through the most desolate landscape yet. As we moved south, the terrain got more sparsely populated with each border. I checked the GPS. It was about thirty miles to Choluteca. We couldn't get there fast enough.

"Did we get fleeced or robbed?" Dean finally asked. "I'm not sure if that was just your typical scam or something that could have been much worse."

"I'm not sure either, but what's the difference?" Still a little frayed, I appreciated that I had not been terrified, and we hadn't panicked. Somehow, we got out of there. I looked out over the golden, barren hills of the Choluteca Plain.

●   ●   ●

I knew a little about this area, at least scientifically. It had been analyzed by hydrologists worldwide after Hurricane Mitch in 1998. Mitch was the biggest Atlantic storm of the century, twenty thousand casualties, the majority in Honduras, most of them here. It was the deadliest storm of the century. There wasn't even a close second. The massive rainfall had induced landslides and swollen the local rivers to six times their annual flow. The water cascading off the hills, stripped of trees for agriculture centuries before, literally swept away the topsoil and towns, turning the region into a soaking desert. Thirty percent of the population became homeless instantly.

Through the dust-blown hinterland, we crossed several rivers and passed a few grungy small towns, each a collection of untidy shacks and a few dogs that chased us, their lifespans likely measured in weeks, if not days. There was nothing to induce a stop, and we finally approached Choluteca.

We spotted a pretty nice hotel just outside of town. Inside, I explained our situation. The hotel clerk and maintenance man showed us a 240-volt socket on a pole behind the hotel. I checked the power and wiring. It was good, but as I removed the charging adapter from the trunk, the hotel clerk returned.

In Spanish, he said, "The owner doesn't want you to charge."

Dean began to protest.

My shirt drenched in sweat, my body drained, my mind devoid of humor, I took a final drag from my cigarette, dropped it on the ground, and turned to Dean. "Let's go check out the Rivera, and whatever else is here. If we don't find anything, we'll come back and bribe this son of a bitch. Everybody's got a price. I need to get some more money anyway."

I turned to the clerk. *"Dónde está el Hotel Rivera?"*

"Across the bridge," he said in Spanish, pointing. "Take a left at the town's only red light. You will see it."

Off we went, over the destructive Choluteca River, and across the town's only sight, the eight hundred-foot suspension bridge built by the US Army Corps of Engineers and the famous bridge engineer Conde B. McCullough, in the 1930s. It had survived Mitch. Maybe the Corps should employ the same safety factors to levees around New Orleans.

We haphazardly drove around town, but found no red light and saw little, really not much more than a village with dust-covered streets, many playing out to dirt not far off the main drag. The scenery was simple, single-story wood or stucco buildings under tile roofs. We found ourselves in a residential neighborhood, the yards filled with clothes drying over taut metal wires.

In Central America, there are no phone-data services. It's not like Orlando, where you can google for hotels or map an address. We just moseyed along on a journey of discovery, like nineteenth-century explorers, but in a fast car and watching the GPS map our location relative to the city's boundaries and major streets.

We finally returned to the town's main intersection, where the Pan American Highway had a stop sign. A stop sign must be called a red light locally. Taking a left, we found the Rivera. Not too bad. I went in, spreading around the few American dollars I had left in my clothes bag. Soon, we viewed the rooms. Inside, they had ACs powered by 240-volt juice. After checking in, we powered up. The AC was high up on the wall, and Dean made a sling and tied it to the AC to hold up the heavy extension cord. We ran the cord through the room's window. It would be a steamy night in Honduras without air conditioning.

I went across the street to a grocery store, a Latin madhouse where I sucked three hundred dollars worth of Honduran lempiras from an ATM and bought some water, chips, and cheap Central American cigarettes. The Super Bowl started in ten minutes. I didn't have a favorite, but hoped the Broncos might pull it off. Peyton Manning is from Louisiana, and the thug Seahawks had knocked the Saints out of the playoffs a few weeks earlier.

By the time I got back to the room, we had popped the fuse. I found the hotel's maintenance man, tipped him, and after fifteen or twenty minutes found the 20-amp fuse and reset it. I was learning, begrudgingly, that for some reason, the Central American fuses tripped on much smaller amperages than in the States—just another variable to consider in this comic escapade.

I lowered the charging rate to 13 amps and did a quick calculation. We'd get 117 miles of charge by six-thirty the next morning. With the 100 miles we still had in the tank, we'd hopefully get somewhere.

It had been a long nine hours that day. We'd gone 185 miles. I finally flopped down on the bed to give my attention to the TV. The Spanish-language announcers babbled away. Only into the second quarter, the Seahawks were already up three touchdowns. The Super Bowl was essentially over.

As I powered up my computer, Dean walked into the room. "What's up?" I said.

Dean put his hands on his hips. "Is there something in that electric car's manual that says it will not charge unless you've got your shirt off? After all we've been through, why do you insist on torturing me in these cramped quarters, showing off your big white belly."

I lifted my computer, setting it on my bare but sweaty stomach and checked a few emails. "We may be starting to get noticed. Bill Moore with *EV World* wants to do a conference call with us. He sent me the number to call him." I looked at my cell phone. I had service, but it was low. I hit reply and typed out a response.

> Thanks Bill. We're in rural Honduras now. Tomorrow, I will likely have some better phone service. Tomorrow around 6 will be good. I'll email to confirm an hour earlier. If you don't hear from me, we got caught up on the road somewhere, but I will touch base with you the next time I have email service. Best, Randy

Impatient for morning, I scratched out a few notes from the day and answered an email or two, my body dying to fall asleep. I had days earlier given up writing, too busy just taking care of the essentials. We were out on a limb, for sure, but hopefully at the bottom of the cauldron. The trip was somewhat like a pendulum. With the exception of northern Mexico, the countries got worse, at least from a wealth and safety perspective. But from here, they should progressively get better and more modern.

• • •

The trip had started with fanciful romance, a fantastic excursion, a break from the real world. It had now devolved into something more like work, the days and nights filled only with the cumbersome job of getting there, with little else to occupy our minds. In our quest to daily keep moving south, the scenery and exotic locales had almost unnoticeably turned bland. But we might actually make it to Panama if we could get through Honduras.

I picked up the map, having little clue what lay ahead. The ominous, now everyday question besieged me. Where were we going, and what lay ahead?

• • •

With daylight, we said goodbye to Choluteca. Late in the night, we'd apparently blown the fuse again, but we did have 188 miles of battery. As Dean complained about the local beer, we slipped out of town, stopping at a military checkpoint only to be waved along by the friendly sergeant after producing our papers. The Nicaraguan border was only forty miles away. I wanted to get there early. We hoped to make Granada, the ancient Spanish city on the banks of Lake Nicaragua.

Though we'd had little correspondence with the Honduran natives, with the exception of the border villains, most were smiling and eager to help. The night before, an English-speaking Honduran gentlemen staying at the hotel had knocked on our door, wanting to look at the car he'd heard about. We showed the fifty-ish man the car, all its bells and whistles, and he took a few pictures. I bartered for some directions, and he told us the best way to Managua, Nicaragua's capital, was to get off of the Pan American Highway onto CA-3, via Somotillo, closer to the coast.

We conversed with the man, a professional, for a good hour, and told him our story of the latest border crossing. He lamented and explained the dire state of his beloved country, large portions of it now overrun with narco cutthroats in bed with the government.

The man (I won't mention his name, profession, or city) told us the sad story of his own plight. Recently extorted for money he couldn't pay, he was currently applying for a work visa in Canada. The criminals had, out of the blue, paid him a visit, saying they knew everything about him, where he lived, where his kids went to school, what type of car his wife drove, etc. The local police had told him they couldn't help.

• • •

Stories like this remind me how fortunate we are in America, or how simple corruption can corrode every facet of society. Later in the night, I watched two large Honduran families lounging and playing around the hotel's pool. The cute kids splashed in and out of the refreshing water as the parents laughed and sipped drinks at a table.

I've always thought Central American families are much closer than American families, probably because of the lack of a social net. The family is all they have. And we have little concept of the stress these families live with every day—their son might accidentally end up in the wrong place at the wrong time, their beautiful young daughter might catch the eye of a powerful gangster, or a family member could just disappear.

In the States, it doesn't matter if you're the local whiz kid who went on to found a software company or you went to work at the local mill at eighteen and ended up a foreman twenty years later. If you've been an honest, productive citizen, you've built up some capital with the community. You get the benefit of the doubt, and you typically have to do something wrong to get sideways with the government or underworld.

The opposite holds true in much of the third world. The more successful you are, at least until you become the very rare super-rich, the more you become vulnerable, a target. Here, I'm constantly reminded that it's not America's affluence that makes it rich, but the rule of law. Without it, nothing else matters, and nothing will bear more fruit than for humankind to live with the rules of the game established and adhered to. No amount of government aid, handouts, or pork can match this, so sought after in much of the world but taken for granted daily at home.

Honduras appeared totally broken. Though statistics vary, it's probably the poorest, most lawless country in Central America. The security situation has devolved so much in recent years that in 2012, the Peace Corps, present in the country since its inception in 1961, pulled out citing security concerns.

The country has avoided the modern outright civil wars that have infected its neighbors in the last hundred years, but minor conflicts between leftists and the government never seem to end. Largely democratic for more than twenty years, things have not worked out so well for Honduras and its eight million residents, almost all of mixed European and indigenous descent.

The American influence has been similar to everywhere else in the region, the country dominated by United Fruit, only to be followed by CIA-trained military dictatorships and death squads to beat off the Communists. In the 1980s, America funded a proxy army here known as the Contras to fight off Central American leftists. Of course, like the Communists they battled, the Contras cut off a few innocent heads and raped a few women along the way despite the fact they were backed by one of the world's most civil nations. Even in 2009, the Honduran Congress had removed the president in an act condemned by most of the world.

A few months later, to show who was still in charge, the narcos had the country's hardline antidrug czar, General Julian Aristides Gonzalez, gunned down after he dropped his daughter off at school.

The Southern writer O. Henry coined the term Banana Republic after a stay in Honduras a hundred years ago. Today, I was ready to put the place behind us. I'd been to Honduras on several occasions in the last decade, and even driven across a large section of it, although under the care of an Interpol agent. But traveling to the Bay Islands or the touristy Mayan ruins of Copán is not the Honduras most of the natives experience every day.

• • •

Awash with natural beauty, smiling eyes, cultural riches, and colonial plazas all begging to be discovered, the country has the potential to be a travelers' paradise. But the possibilities of the country are far from the realities of today, and forsaken southwestern Honduras is no place to hang out and sightsee in a shiny new car that you can't fill up at the local gas station.

Just before the Nicaraguan border, we passed through the little town of Guasaule. With just a few hundred people, it had only five or six dirt side streets, sided by run-down, tin-roofed buildings. These little impoverished villages all look docile. Two months after we passed through Guasaule I read a story that the local authorities had found a young Honduran man, his head lopped off, lying in the muddy streets.

As we said goodbye to Hondurans, I hoped, maybe with our sincere help one day, the country would get this all sorted out so their kids could grow up to be safe and successful, possibly even so bored with their easy lives, they'd want to ride off into the unknown somewhere just to get a break from their humdrum schedule.

Poets, Volcanoes,
and Hugo Chavez

Getting out of Honduras was a hell of lot easier than getting in. The border crossing had a few hawkers and handlers, but we brushed off the hooligans and stamped out of the country a little after 8:00 a.m.. We made it. Across the Rio Guasaule we went, greeted politely by the first Nicaraguan border guard.

"Welcome to Nicaragua," he said in English.

I presented my papers and after a few questions was motioned forward.

I turned to Dean, surprised at the simplicity. "Maybe this won't be so bad."

"Don't count your chickens yet."

"I've been here before," I said. "Much better than Honduras. It's the land of volcanoes and poets." I raised our guidebook. "*Lonely Planet* concurs. Poetry is the national pastime. Even the Communists and right-wing generals consider themselves poets."

We found the immigration building, bothered only by three young kids. In fact, the Nicaraguans, or Nicas as they call themselves, had a novel plan to promote tourism—a policeman pacing the area to run off anyone pestering us. He asked us about the kids, but I said, "*No problemo.*" Maybe I'd been overcritical of big government.

We processed all the paperwork in less than an hour. The three little kids, not even ten years old, led us around, pointing and mumbling, "Over there."

Dean bought the little businessmen a Coke, and I exchanged some of my Honduran lempiras for Nicaraguan cordobas as I wondered why the future villains weren't in school learning to read and add. The other good news was the crossing was still too complicated for Dean to get a driver's permit.

In less than an hour, we were on the open road, a stretch of pavement slicing through the coastal plain. My initial impression was alarm at the number of horses, buggies, and *vaqueros* (cowboys) traversing the road, far more than we'd seen anywhere else.

We plowed on, around a few potholes and through a few no-account villages. These rural Central American towns had all started to look the same—shabby, wooden shacks; dark, affable, and carefree citizens clustered around the road; trash as abundant as grass. Here, the landscape was more open, flat, less verdant, the land parched and sunburned. This wasn't a theme park or parade—the prevalent horses and wagons weren't props, but actually conducted meaningful chores. Still, I couldn't believe the helpful nature of the Nicas and how easily we'd gotten over the border.

• • •

No country should have more disdain for Americans than Nicaragua, as no country has ever had more internal meddling from the Colossus of the North. One of the country's first presidents was a nineteenth-century American adventurer, William Walker, who wrested power from the locals. He was later ousted by the Costa

Ricans and Hondurans, the latter planting him on their eastern shore.

In the first half of the twentieth century, the Marines invaded and occupied the country twice in a twenty-year span, fighting pitched battles with leftist guerrillas. Famous Marines like Roy Geiger, Joseph Henry Pendleton, Chesty Puller, and Merritt "Red Mike" Edson cut their teeth chasing leftists or their colorful leader, Augusto Sandino, the Central American version of George Washington. (Of course, George Washington won his revolution.) Marine General Smedley Butler later claimed:

> I helped purify Nicaragua for the International Banking House of Brown Brothers in 1902-1912.

A little note on Chesty Puller. He has a famous quote that brings back fond memories of my days in the military. Forced to review a bunch of dressed-up, uninspired Marines, maybe here in Nicaragua, he uttered the timeless words: "Take me to the brig. I want to see the real Marines."

The future generals were hard on the imperialist Japanese, but they never caught Sandino. For that, we installed a military dictator who finished the job. General Anastasio Somoza García and his sons ruled the country for the next fifty years.

Their regime was one of the most authoritarian and brutal of the twentieth century until the Sandinista Nicaraguans (named after Sandino) threw them out, and the United States hired the Contras to undo this in the 1980s. For more than a hundred years, much of the fighting was here, in the north around the liberal bastions of Chinandega and León.

Why America has interfered so often in Central America is open to debate. Every scholar has an opinion. Surely, some of it was due to imperialistic motives. More probable is the vain idealism of Rudyard Kipling's poem more than a century old, "The White Man's Burden" —though it might be costly and burdensome, it is the "civilized" white man's obligation to force our "superior" system on the uncivilized brown people for their benefit. Henry Kissinger had a more pragmatic view in the midst of the Cold War:

> I don't see why we need to stand by and watch a country go communist due to the irresponsibility of its own people.

·   ·   ·

We drove on, the citizens scarce and land opening up, row crops and grassland becoming rampant. We passed through Reserva Genéticos Apacunca, one of the few remaining wild cornfields on the planet.

An hour into Nicaragua and through the miles of sugarcane, we passed through Chinandega. The fertile volcanic soil around the city is some of the richest in the Americas. The heat and rainfall produce bountiful cotton, sugercane, and oranges. Chinandegans shouldn't like us here either. During the Marine Corps incursion of the 1920s, much of the town was gutted by American flying mercenaries

On and on we went, around the cars, potholes, horses, and volcanoes, down the old rail corridor. Nicaragua's railroads, built in the 1880s by the famous American rail engineers Henry Meiggs and Minor Keith, who constructed many of the railroads in the Andes, and John Edward Hollenbeck, an early developer of Los Angeles, are sadly no longer in service. Constructed only fifteen years after the American Transcontinental Railroad, they were ripped up a decade ago, the steel sold for scrap.

In Chichigalpa, we passed the distillery for the famous Nicaraguan rum, Flor de Caña (Flower of the Cane), and possibly the oldest sugarcane mill in the world, Ingenio San Antonio, first noted by the French pirate William Dampier in 1685.

Cautiously studying the range meter, we rolled through León. Founded along with Granada in 1524 by the Spaniard Francisco Hernández de Córdoba as one of the country's two principal cities, León, called the white city for its adobe buildings, is known for its liberalism. The ruling powers of the city and the conservative stronghold Granada have been at each other's throats for almost five hundred years. It's not so much a rich-versus-poor thing, as it's mostly rich conservatives against rich liberals, kind of like America. Once the country's capital, the crumbling colonial beauty was home to Nicaragua's most famous poet, Rubén Darío. It was also here, in 1956, that the poet Rigoberto López Pérez shot and killed the American puppet dictator, General Anastasio Somoza García.

Actually, this isn't even the original León. The city's been moved, the residents tired of rebuilding it due to Volcano Momotombo's perpetual activity.

We made a left in León, the road to Granada going right by Old León, a World Heritage Site eighteen miles away. We were making such good time, I thought we might stop and check it out, but a few miles outside of León we hit a hitch. The road was closed for construction. There was no re-route. It simply dead-ended. You would think there'd be a sign somewhere in León, "Road Closed Ahead," "Don't Go this Way," whatever!

I pulled over, alarm bells going off in my brain. With the limited charging the night before, we were cutting it close today—the closest of the trip. Our goal was Granada, 185 miles from Choluteca. We started the day with 188 miles of EPA range, probably actually a tad over 200 miles with our slow pace. We didn't have much room for error.

We checked our maps. The night before I'd found a few hotels in Granada where I thought we could get a charge. Correlating the GPS with the maps, we deliberated. There was another road out of León. It would add about twenty miles to our trip. This, and the extra driving getting here and back to León ruled out Granada. Scanning the maps, we decided on Managua, the country's capital. We could make it there, but with little spare juice. We couldn't afford another wrong turn or construction detour. I exhaled a long breath. We had no other options except León.

We hastened back to León and across the rolling terrain. Dean diligently held the map and studied the GPS to make sure we stayed on course.

"If something doesn't look right," I said, lighting up, "we'll stop and sort it out. We don't have enough spare power for even a small wrong turn."

"Relax. I got it under control. You just smoke your nasty-ass Honduran cigarettes and drive."

We passed volcano after volcano, four or five in a thirty-mile span, a few smoking pretty good. It's hard to convey the quantity of volcanoes on this portion of the planet. In the last 350 miles, we had driven by more than forty *active* volcanoes. That stretch of road is about the same as the distance from Los Angeles to San Francisco, Chicago to St. Louis, or Washington DC to Boston.

Even for a flatlander like me, the novelty of seeing volcanos wore off after our first day in Guatemala, but Nicaragua's volcanos are different—much more splendid, probably because they sit on the somewhat flat ground of the coastal step, penetrating the sky above fluttering golden fields. They're everywhere, and you motor so close you can see the steep, symmetrical slopes collide with the land as you drive through their shadows. What a strange and exotic experience. I felt utter excitement for the first time in days.

We drove past the magnificent Volcano Momotombo, along the shore of the four hundred-square-mile Lake Managua. Like many in Central America, it also serves as a toilet and swimming was not recommended.

On to Ciudad Sandino and into Managua, as Dean searched the GPS for hotels, finding only the Crowne Plaza. He punched it in.

Looking at the GPS, I made a left turn from the wrong lane. A local street cop pulled me over, determined to write me a ticket.

I took Dean's advice, acting dumb. To every inquiry, I simply presented my passport and driver's permit, muttering, "*Norte Americano, no hablo Español.*"

The officers spoke among themselves, scribbling on their ticket-pad.

I didn't want to get a ticket. No telling what it would entail to pay it.

They asked a few more questions. "What is your local address?" etc.

I continued to play dumb.

Finally exhausted and probably realizing this was more trouble than it was worth, the officer wadded up the paper, shook his finger at me, and motioned us on.

Trying to follow the GPS, I darted through Managua and its more than two million residents, a large portion crammed onto the winding, tree-lined city streets. Wrong turn after wrong turn, we made our way to the Crowne Plaza.

Driving in Managua is the motorized equivalent of running with the bulls in Spain. The city's been razed by earthquakes so many times, it has no center or grid, just a labyrinth of mesmerizing streets that cut through the jungle, or through the shambles of a one-time market or neighborhood. Guidebooks have entire sections dedicated to navigating the city, since Mother Nature's disruptions have left it virtually without street addresses. You find your way around literally by compass, with addresses referencing distances and directions from a lake, monument, or "something else." If that "something else" was destroyed in an earthquake, well, stop and ask someone.

Into the brouhaha we went. I was getting used to Central American driving, more akin to wrestling that entails a lot of smoking, honking, and rude gestures, requiring only the finger that the natives rely on, like a rolling soccer game. Here, tailgating appeared to be the national sport, and a few times I wondered if I'd missed the sign that said we were now supposed to drive on the left side of the road.

I finally turned off the volume on the GPS, tired of it telling me to take a left when there was no road. At the numerous red lights, we got a break and a chance to take in the cauldron of urban disorder, ruckus, noise, and dirty streets, where Western comforts sat alongside third-world poverty. I saw the unimaginable, a mother riding a moped with a baby cradled in her arms, and a few cars bellowing smoke so thick that back home, even in Louisiana, the environmental police would be ready to lock the poor drivers up and turn the cars into metal shreds.

A bus was crammed so tight, a half-dozen people hung out of the doors and windows. Pedestrians of every sort mingled along the road. It's always amazed me that, despite the relative poverty here, beggars and street dangers are significantly less visible than in much wealthier places. Income levels in New York's Garment District are some of the highest in the world, but a stroll around Penn Station might lead a stranger to think that half the population is either homeless or hardened criminals. Here, everyone looks friendly.

Then we saw Hugo, Hugo Chavez that is, decorated with thousands of golden light bulbs. The gigantic steel mural sat in the middle of a large traffic circle, now known as *Hugo Chávez Eternal Comandante Rotonda*. The monument was recently erected by America's longtime nemesis, Daniel Ortega, the current president and onetime arch-enemy of Ronald Reagan. A hard-boiled Communist in the 1970s and '80s, he's moderated his views to accommodate the new world order, a mix of capitalism, socialism, and democracy. And yes, he's a poet too.

Through the ruckus of traffic, Dean saw the Crowne Plaza poking up above the tall trees and buildings.

I still didn't know how to get there. We motored into the traffic circle and were swept around Hugo, dumped off on a side street going the wrong way. We did pass an eerie testament to Managua's past, the Tribune Monumental, built by the Somoza regime as a huge stone grandstand for watching military parades. Now defaced and strewn with weeds, it resembled some of the Nazis' viewing structures for rallies—once the center of a country's attention, but now hidden away in disrepair, only visited by tourists, an everlasting reminder of the country and its leaders' sins.

Tired of going nowhere, we parked, and Dean took off on foot to find the route. In this maze of concrete, the simplest form of exploration is the one that often works.

Through the Lobby

Down to thirty miles of range, I pulled into the Crowne Plaza, ten stories of concrete shaped like a pyramid. If nothing else, it likely had an English speaker who could help us find a charge. I scanned the parking area, looking for the mechanical room, then studied the lobby, scrutinizing the available power.

We were learning the art of charging as we went, and my recent education taught me to look for something that might work before talking to the hotel staff. This would help my cause and reduce the turmoil. I could show them what I needed instead of asking them. The Crowne Plaza didn't look promising. The hotel had central air. Everything was 120 volts, and if it had a mechanical area, it was hidden away somewhere.

More importantly, I'd discovered a few key points that produced positive results when haggling with locals for power: be persistent, convey a sense of doom, and *muchas propinas* (liberal tipping).

I explained our situation to the polite young woman at the front desk, and she relayed our problem to the manager, a man about my age who spoke terrific English.

I was soon walking the grounds with three of the hotel's maintenance crew, including the resident electrician. I showed him the car, and he spent fifteen minutes admiring it and taking a few pictures. I had discovered that lifting the hood to show there was no engine produced the biggest effect, often inducing a jumble of quick Spanish. Today was no different.

"*De Texas a aquí*," I said. "*No gasolina.*"

The electrician's eyes and smile got big. "Yes?"

I pulled out some cash, twenty American. The Latin eyes got bigger. I showed the electrician all my extension cords and the charging adapter. "*Doscientos cuarenta voltios.*"

The electrician pondered a few seconds, rubbing his hands together. He then led Dean and me into the hotel's convention center across the street. We walked through the grand lobby, the ballroom, and then down some steps to a little room filled with wires.

The electrician pointed to the breaker box, illuminating it with a flashlight.

I surveyed the boxes and wires, but saw no socket.

He pointed to two big wires, dead-ending out of the fuse box. "*Doscientos cuarenta voltios.*"

I studied the situation, calculating. I raised my hand, putting my thumb and index finger close together. "*Un momento.*"

I stepped back and gauged the distance from the street through the lobby and ballroom to the electrical room. Our two hundred-foot extension cord would likely reach here. If not, I had another one hundred-foot cord we could add to the end of it. I walked to the car, got my plug bag, grabbed one of the plug adapters that fit the extension cord and removed the male end, leaving the three leads exposed. I grabbed the Tesla's charging adapter, my flashlight, and the plug, and strolled back to the electrical room.

With amazement, Dean and I watched the electrician wire us up directly to the breaker box. In no time, we plugged in the adapter and got a green. We then pulled the car in front of the convention center and stretched the cord through the lobby, jamming it under one of the eight 16-foot-tall glass doors. We were charging at 25 amps. The traveling circus was in business. We'd be fully charged by five in the morning.

I shook everyone's hand. The hotel staff laughed and joked, full of Latin carefree bliss. The maintenance crew seemed to enjoy the madness more than we did.

Checking in, I inquired about the hotel doing our laundry, not cleaned since we left Texas, and in dire need of some soap and water.

"*Sí*," the young woman at the front desk said with a smile.

I pointed to my watch. "*Este noche. Vamos muy temprano in la mañana.*"

"Yes, by seven or eight tonight," she said in English. "There are some fine cafés and bars near the hotel. Would you like some suggestions?"

"Maybe later," I said, taken aback by how friendly and helpful all the Communists were, especially to such an obvious imperialist.

Utilizing the hotel's business center, I emailed Bill Moore, of *EV World*, and after a brief exchange of emails, we set the interview for six that night. I looked at my watch, a twenty-five-dollar Timex that I'd bought in basic training more twenty-five years ago. It had been around the world with me several times, through a war, across oceans, to mountain summits, and everywhere in between. It still ticked away, accurate as a Rolex.

It was only a little after two. We'd covered the 180 miles, including the border crossing and the dead-end side trip in just under eight hours. Not like a drive down I-20 from Shreveport to Dallas, but pretty good for Central America. More importantly, for the first time since leaving Mexico, we were charging with some sunlight left in the day to relax or take care of much-needed chores.

I walked back outside. By now, a half-dozen Nicas stood around the car, inspecting the strange machine. I later discovered that the English-language newspaper in Managua had done a brief story about the electric car passing through the country's capital.

With its strange shape, the hotel itself, formerly the Hotel Intercontinental, was something of an historical landmark. Perched high in the Barrio Martha Quezada, it sat only a few blocks from most of the government buildings. Just down the hill was a park and the site of the old Casa Presidencial, where the Somoza gang executed the revolutionary Augusto Sandino in 1934. One of the few buildings to survive the massive 1972 earthquake that killed six thousand, injured twenty thousand, and left another quarter million homeless, the hotel has over the years hosted such famous guests as Howard Hughes, dozens of foreign journalists during the revolution of the 1980s, and even the Sandinista government at one time.

Managua was founded with little planning, a compromise capital between Granada and León, which were always fighting. Of course, they didn't have seismologists then. The city sits almost exactly on a tectonic fault line, the intersection of the Cocos and Caribbean Plates. It's been destroyed twice in the last century, 1931 and 1972.

Seismologists say the city remains at a high risk today, the frequency of the big ones roughly fifty years apart. It's been forty-two years since the '72 quake, almost the exact time between the '31 and '72 quakes. Maybe we could get out of town before the city fell down around us.

•   •   •

I had some tasks to tend to. Most notably, it was time to refill my pillbox. Have I told the reader that since reaching my forties, my body has started to fall apart? I've been lucky in one regard. I often pass for someone in his thirties. On the flip side, I sometimes feel like I'm sixty-five. Yes, there are a lot of miles on me after three decades of sin and pleasure, but you can't take the organs with you—might as well use them up.

I'm a Southern Baptist, at least by birth, and in fact do have some things in common with Southern Baptists. Southern Baptists like to drink on the back porch. I like to drink on the back and front porches. There are also some major differences. Southern Baptists have some strict social norms. I myself can think of nothing good associated with the word "chastity."

Have no doubt—I am a Christian. I just believe in a more contemporary type of salvation. I prefer to ask for forgiveness. Actually, if it weren't for sinners needing to repent, there'd be no need for churches or preachers.

But my liberal lifestyle is beginning to wear on my strong Southern bones, and now, in my mid-forties, the cold reality that I'm mortal is hitting home. Hangovers used to take hours to get over, now they take days. I've been to the doctor more in the last few years than the entire first forty.

I dug through the car for my now essential travel companion, something most everybody over eighty has, my two-week pillbox. A few years ago, I was diagnosed with rheumatoid arthritis. To date, the doctors seem positive, and I've felt few effects outside of occasional morning stiffness. My life is generally unchanged except for the daily ritual that is my concoction of pills.

I dumped the last of the tablets in my hand, tossed them in my mouth, and gulped down the remnants of a sixteen-ounce water bottle. The directions with some of the drugs instruct me to consume them with light food. Hell, some of the pills are breakfast, the size of mini-sausage links.

Aside from my official medical conditions, I have the typical problems of most aging men. Even before my diagnosis, just the slightest indulgence packed on the weight. A good, long weekend might add six pounds to my beer- and pizza-belly.

My new dose of steroids daily, though very small, puts fat on me at a new and alarming rate. Merely looking at a cheeseburger adds a pound. Now, anything appetizing adds to my mass at almost the actual weight of the food. A sixteen-ounce sandwich with any trimmings seems to add sixteen ounces to my overblown spare tire.

I live the utterly miserable life of a twenty-year-old runway model: daily exercise, eating like a parrot, and hopping on and off the scales three or four times a day. Try that in Louisiana where everything from shish-kabob to green beans is fried or dipped in some coon-ass sauce that makes butter seem like diet food. Hanky-panky for me nowadays is with my shirt on, at least until the lights are off.

All of this weighs on my mind, though thankfully not constantly, at least not yet. Literally, painfully, I'm getting older, and the reality is I don't have plenty of years left to do some of the things we've all taken for granted. I don't mean to be fatalistic, but it seems like yesterday I was just out of college, but in the last year alone, I've twice had the awkward job of scrolling down my phone's contacts to delete a name. That takes your breath away.

My body drained, dehydration cramping my calves, my stomach turning woozy from my prescribed snack, I dug around the car for a can of Pringles I'd bought the day before. The bright midday sun reflecting off the white car shot into my eyes. Did I mention my eyes have gone too, probably from decades of staring at a computer screen? I can see next to nothing at less than a foot, and even the mildest light makes me squint. I paraded over beaches and crossed deserts all over the world in my youth and never even knew what sunglasses were until I was forty. Now, I find myself reaching for them in traffic at dusk. What a pansy I've become.

· · ·

The chips weren't in the car. Dean's sorry ass must have eaten them. I didn't really care. I looked over to a mall beside the hotel, then to the tumultuous streets, a boiling pot of life and energy. Under the thick canopy of green trees and exquisite Spanish buildings, the reinvented Nicaragua displayed itself proudly—urban, but also old-world, decaying and shiny, fast-paced, but not in a hurry. Two old men in Panama hats argued as three tall, curvy Nicaraguan beauties strolled by in high heels, their long, dark hair flowing and their faces partially hidden by big, chic sunshades.

I had time to goof off and relax. I'd go get something to eat, enjoy the Nicas and Managua, fumble around and explore while I could. This time tomorrow, no telling what kind of debacle we might fight through in hopes of getting us and the white sedan down the road.

In Mr. Twain's Footsteps

By eight the next morning the car was fully charged. The previous evening, the charging had popped another breaker. This really confounded me because it was 40 amps. It was not a big deal, right beside our cord, and I reset it and lowered the charging to 18 amps. The blowing fuses were a good thing, an indication that the power grid had ample safeguards, but they wreaked havoc on our sleep. We were now forever getting up during the night to make sure the car was charging.

The phone interview the evening before with *EV World* and Bill Moore went well, probably almost an hour. Our story astonished and baffled the EV expert. Bill recorded almost thirty minutes of it and said he would put the story and a podcast up on his web page the next day.

That night, my heart rate settled down for the first time in days, and I had a chance to mull over what we'd accomplished—driving two thousand road-miles south of the United States in an electric car. A part of me couldn't believe we'd actually made it this far. Barring a wreck or theft, we'd likely make it to Panama. The reality of it all was hard to grasp, my mind numb, the last few weeks like a rush, a dream, something not quite real.

A peaceful calm sank over me as I plotted the next day's trip. I spent little time trying to figure out how to get out of Managua. The Calle Colon beside the hotel went to Masaya. If we made a wrong turn, we'd just work our way south until we got back on the right road.

Planning for the day's drive required an approach similar to preparing for a military operation. It doesn't really matter how much planning you do, as soon as you hit the ground everything goes to pot, and you're left with a bunch of false assumptions and changing circumstances. Having options available is the best course. In the end, we'd get there like the Army got most of its important things done, with American ingenuity and a can-do spirit. We'd improvise. In our case, we'd just keep going south. That was the only plan, and to date, it appeared to be working.

As I checked out of the hotel, the manager who spoke perfect English, Eduardo, told me the price for the charging was 150 dollars. Actually, this wasn't that bad after how well we'd been treated—the laundry, the use of the business center, and the hotel posting a guard to watch the car. Considering the pinch we'd been in and applying basic economic laws of supply and demand, 1,000 dollars would have probably been the market value. Still, I decided to haggle a little—150 dollars for 10 dollars worth of electricity was a little over the top.

I produced a big smile. "Eduardo, you've been watching too much American TV. I'm not a movie star or internet millionaire. Just a regular American."

With a shiny bald head and warm grin, he rolled his eyes at me. "What do you think is fair?"

"Only cost about ten dollars in the States." I motioned to the computer. "Look it up."

Another young man appeared beside Eduardo, taking interest in the conversation. The two conversed briefly in Spanish.

It was time to pitch in, aid our new Nicaraguan friends in their reinvention—a lesson in capitalism. I gently slapped my hands together. "How about fifty dollars? I purchased one of the hotel's suites and have already spread another forty around to the staff. This will work out fine. We got a much-needed service. And the staff and the Crowne Plaza will make a nice profit. And I will be out of your hair and off to see Masaya."

The two men looked at each other, each thinking silently before Eduardo made a few short, quick nods. "Okay, that is good."

We made it out of Managua with only one wrong turn, passing a lot of churches and parks, and even a baseball field. The churches and plazas had all long since started to look the same, but not the baseball diamond, an everlasting testament to American intrusion here. So great was our presence in the last century that baseball instead of soccer is the national sport. I inventoried some of the buildings, many looking like they were only an earthquake away from cinders. Central American building and electrical codes must be similar.

On the road, we made another wrong turn in Masaya, forced to drive down the lakefront during the morning rush hour. Every form of life and mechanical equipment competed for space on the tight road. Off to our left, perched on a high hill, the stone fortress of Coyotepe watched over the town.

A century earlier, in a storied assault, American Marines stormed the hill and took the fortress, killing one of the country's first revolutionaries, General Benjamín Zeledón. His body was then thrown in an oxcart and paraded through Masaya on its way to a cemetery south of town, probably via the main street's ageless brick road that we now bounced over.

We did get a brief glimpse of the caldera lake that protects the city from the active Volcano Masaya. Just outside of town, you can actually drive up to the rim of the Santiago Crater and look down at the bubbling lava pool constantly venting sulfur dioxide, called the "mouth of hell" by the Spaniards. I'd heard that if the wind is right, you can smell the sulfur in town, but all I got a whiff of was the manure from the horse-drawn buggies.

Dean turned up some rock and roll—AC/DC thudded from the Tesla as we rolled through town.

"Dude," I said, "put on something more mellow. Like maybe Frank Sinatra. We may attract some gangsters. Not to mention the fucking headache you're giving me."

Dean turned his camera to a distant volcano. "Nicaragua's the coolest place we've been. Ain't no gangsters here. And I might get some good footage of that volcano if I could ever film just one minute without you dropping every curse word you know. I'd like to be able to show some of this to my mother."

"At least you've gotten out from behind the wheel to film. And if anybody understands my issues, it's your mom."

"My filming behind the wheel wasn't any worse than your driving and digging around for your cigarettes, or gum, or potato chips."

Back on the road, we passed through Nandaime, moved here hundreds of years ago when the original town was buried in a landslide from the nearby Volcano Mombacho. The land here is active, an integral part of the changing times. I feel for the civil engineers here. I thought being a flood-control engineer in Louisiana was bad enough with large portions of the state below sea level and water assailing us not only from the hurricanes, but also the thirty-one states that drain into the Mississippi River. Here, they had hurricanes, volcanoes, landslides, and earthquakes. I bet everybody bitched at the engineers.

Back on the Pan American Highway, the land beside the road got more rural by the mile. We scooted on to Rivas through mango

trees and parakeets, the landscape morphing into broken, windswept plains spiked with volcanoes, and covered with a patchwork
of farms and ranches.

The isolated splendor of the rugged landscape evoked a
placid delight. Though populated, humankind's mark on the land
was minimal. Overlanding here, I never got the sense that I might
stumble out of the bush and onto an interstate, the sound and sight
of cars and cargo rushing to be somewhere breaking me from a
surreal trance.

We finally moved onto the shore of Lake Nicaragua, the tenth-
biggest lake in the Western hemisphere and home to the planet's
only freshwater sharks. This area had long been cherished by Americans. During the 1849 Gold Rush, Cornelius Vanderbilt operated
a shipping company to get Americans from the East Coast to California. The mogul ran steamships up Nicaragua's San Juan River
and across Lake Nicaragua, requiring only a fifteen-mile overland
trip to reach the Pacific.

This was also the area of the first proposed canal joining the
oceans. In 1885, the US Navy sent the renowned hydraulic engineer A. G. Menocal here for an official survey.

Feeling liberated, I drove with less urgency than in previous
days. The *topes* all but gone, I reveled in the exploration of the
unknown road ahead, especially via such a rare means of transport.
For as long as I can remember, I've been fascinated with famous
tales of exploration and discovery, man's conquering of space and
time. The exploits of the world's great explorers—John Fremont,
Teddy Roosevelt, or Richard Burton to name a few, and their
sojourns to the far corners of the world—have always entranced
me.

Against the beautiful, spotless sky, an airliner was on its initial approach over the lake, probably bound for San José, Costa

Rica, 175 miles to the south. The comfortable passengers, relaxing in their leather seats, were likely enjoying a book, watching a movie, or sipping wine. They'd be safely there in fifteen or twenty minutes. It would likely take us seven to nine hours of hard battling overland, if we were lucky, to get to San José. What a contrast.

On the banks of the lake, ten miles from the Costa Rican border, we drove through the huge Amayo Wind Farm. The windswept Isthmus of Rivas has some the highest sustained winds in the world, funneling off Lake Nicaragua to the Pacific, their average speed almost 30 mph. I've driven through some of the wind farms in western Texas and outside of Palm Springs, but this one looked bigger, probably because of the linear length and narrow width.

The wind howled today. Talk about cool. We drove right under the gigantic turbines, heard their gears grind, the shadows of their blades racing across the road. We stopped to take a picture. I guess the Americans aren't the only ones tired of giving away their wealth to power their toasters.

Off to our left sat Ometepe Island, with its two 5,000-foot volcanoes. Somewhere to our right was San Juan del Sur, the western point on the old transcontinental crossing. In 1866, Mark Twain crossed right around here on a journey along Mr. Vanderbilt's shortcut. He left to posterity the following description of San Juan del Sur:

> We found San Juan to consist of a few tumble-down frame shanties—they call them hotels—nestling among green verdure and overshadowed by picturesque little hills. The spot where we landed was crowded with horses, mules, ambulances and half-clad yellow natives,

with bowie knives two feet long, and as broad as your hand, strapped to their waists.

And of Ometepe Island:

> Out of the midst of the beautiful Lake Nicaragua spring two magnificent pyramids, clad in the softest and richest green, all flecked with shadow and sunshine, whose summits pierce the billowy clouds. They look so isolated from the world and its turmoil—so tranquil, so dreamy, so steeped in slumber and eternal repose. What a home one might make among their shady forests, their sunny slopes, their breezy dells, after he had grown weary of the toil, anxiety and unrest of the bustling, driving world.

Things haven't changed much in 148 years. As we said goodbye to Nicaragua, I couldn't help but be reminded that it's my favorite of the countries we'd visit. I'd been here once before, but the place is just downright nifty. With few tourists, it's like a huge, untamed park, the vast stretches of wild savanna pockmarked with captivating volcanoes looming over *vaqueros* practicing their trade as they've done for centuries. Between the bush, the ancient Spanish cities teeming with life, good rum, poets, reformed Communists, and the local beauties, real-life versions of Barbara Carrera (the Nicaraguan actress who played the Bond girl Fatima Blush) strolling under the tall palms. Though I've never been, I hear the beaches are some of the best in the world.

Nowhere in Central America is there more promise. If you want to come and see the real Nicaragua, you better come soon. It looks like the Nicas may decide this free-market democracy is to their liking, the gringo money and American lifestyle more important than their way of life. Before long, this place may look like a mix of the Champs Élysées and Woodstock. And of course, this earthquake-prone country would also be better seen before the Big One rattles it back a few centuries.

Just Another
Border Crossing

"Costa Rica here we come," I said as we pulled up to the border crossing. Many Americans experience the dizzying maze of disorder that is a Central American border crossing, but often by bus or taxi, which doesn't include 75 percent of the headache that crossing with a car involves. The crossings make American bureaucracy seem like a fine-oiled machine. Fortunately, the Nicaragua-Costa Rica border crossing on the Pan American Highway is one of the best managed in all of Central America.

Arriving at the Nicaraguan side of the border, we slowly pulled forward through the crowds of people and a few random buildings. We rolled up the windows and locked the doors as the hawkers assaulted us. These sophisticated con men had shirts that were almost identical to the shirts worn by officialdom. The word "Nicaragua" was embroidered on them, but without the government seal. And they had fake badges or cards that looked official, but a close inspection revealed they actually said something like "South Nicaraguan Tourist Company."

We'd learned through experience that typically we had to process out through immigration and then customs. Usually, there are no signs or directions. Today was no different, but we saw a long line, probably fifty people, lined up under a roof behind some bars. That must be immigration.

There was no parking area so we just pulled over on the side of the road. We grabbed all our paperwork (I had two copies of everything made the night before at the Crowne Plaza) and stormed out of the car toward the line of people. The hawkers followed us, babbling away in our faces, and more annoying, constantly grabbing at our passports trying to pull them out of our hands. We got in line.

This border crossing was different than any we'd yet crossed. Half the fifty or so people in line were tourists, European or American. Twenty minutes in line and we got stamped out for a fee of ten American dollars.

I held my driver's permit and showed it to the lady at immigration. "*Tengo un coche.*"

The woman pointed to an office next door. I proceeded there immediately, the hawkers still on my tail. They had stood in line with us at immigration, constantly bothering us. In the mumble and jumble at immigration, I had left my papers on the counter. Terrified, I ran back. Fortunately, they were still there.

In the customs office a man sat behind a desk. I presented my papers.

He complained, "No, no."

I mumbled some Spanish: "*Tengo un coche.*"

The man pointed in the general direction of his right. I went back outside and saw another building where he pointed, but no signs. A man in a uniform was inspecting some luggage. We got in the car and pulled over to the building. There, we got out and approached the man, but he pointed to the building. I went in. The building had five or six offices. I held up my papers to show a guard. He pointed to a door. I went in. A woman sat behind a desk, going over some papers.

"*Perdon*," I said, and held up my papers. "*Tengo un coche.*"

The woman looked at me, groaned, blew out a long breath, and shook her head. She mumbled something and waved me away.

I walked outside, back into the constant murmur of Spanish and general Latin disorder. I wanted to ask someone for guidance, but feared the hawkers. If I asked one of them, we'd never get rid of 'em. I leaned against the car, trying to locate my next option.

A young man who spoke English came out of the building to explain the situation. "The lady inside is busy. You need that man." He pointed to a loading area and a large bus. "But he's checking that bus right now. When he comes back over here, show him your papers."

I lit a cigarette and waited. A dog looked up at me with its tongue hanging out. I had no idea what he wanted, but there are always a lot of dogs hanging out at the border crossings.

Ten minutes later the man arrived. I presented my papers, but he pointed to two uniformed women, leaning against another building. I walked over, offered my papers and pointed to our car. One of the ladies was telling a story to the other lady and a man. She instructed me to wait until she finished. In a few minutes, they laughed at the story, then the ladies followed Dean and me to the car.

The women went over the car real good, asking a bunch of strange questions, half-flirting with us. Everything looked good, but they were in no hurry to sign off. Did they want to flirt some more, or want a tip? Ten minutes later they finally signed and pointed to the first customs building I went to. I went there and waited five minutes behind someone else. I presented the papers and got the stamp.

"*Bueno?*" I asked, pointing south. "Costa Rica?"

"*Sí, sí*," the man said and waved us out of his office.

Getting out of Nicaragua had taken about an hour and a half. In Central America, leaving a country is the easy part. Getting in is much more cumbersome.

We drove through the neutral zone to the Costa Rican border station. There are usually a few side roads utilized by the big trucks or the police, but no signs to lead you. This crossing wasn't that bad, with only one side road where several trucks were parked, so I didn't turn onto it. This crossing had only a half-mile neutral zone, so we arrived at the Costa Rican border station quickly.

All hopes of a quick crossing faded as we saw hundreds of people wandering around the dozen cars or small trucks and three buses. Again, no signs or places to park. A long line of people, more than a hundred, all standing idly, stretched down the road. Probably immigration. We pulled over and parked on the side of the road, locked the car and grabbed our papers to get in line. A man in uniform approached, waving his hands. We couldn't park here. He pointed ahead, to a fence-line off the road where five or six cars were parked. I pulled forward and parked there.

Unfortunately for us, a bus stopped and dumped another fifty or sixty people in the line at immigration. Under a shed, the column weaved around in five or six lanes, like a TSA queue at the airport, then slithered down the road another fifty yards. We joined the procession. It took about forty minutes to get to the door of the immigration building. The only good news was that no hawkers or handlers appeared.

I passed the time smoking and viewing the travelers, more than half of them foreigners, a few tour groups of retirees, and a bunch of backpackers. Some of the tourists look pissed, all bent out of shape about the long wait. I'm thinking: you don't know how lucky you are. You don't have a car. Try this with a flashy new ride without an engine.

We'd been in line for forty-five minutes and in the jungle for weeks. A few of the female backpackers started looking pretty good. I didn't know how often these backpackers bathed, but here, your imagination could run wild. There were two or three I'd certainly like to trade Dean for, especially with some soap, makeup, and a razor. I've never had a mistress with dreadlocks. Could this be the missing link that's kept me from eternal love and happiness all these years? And riding with me would make them famous left-wingers, green crusaders.

As I considered if I should propose, we finally got to the door of the office. Inside, we filled out our paperwork. But we had a problem. We'd filled the paperwork out in pencil. We'd misplaced our pen somewhere. Dean guarded our place inside the building, and I went outside and begged a man for his pen. Back inside, we again waited to fill out our paperwork, this time behind three people.

Finally a stamp. The sound of the stamp thumping against paper is the most beautiful in Latin America. After all the explaining, writing, mulling over papers, conversation between bureaucrats, it's more pleasing to the ears than any Beethoven symphony.

The woman shooed us away, but I asked about customs and the car.

She pointed across the street.

Off we went and found the customs house, just a hut with one agent. I set my papers on the counter and waited a few minutes for him to finish some paperwork. Through all this, I constantly went through my papers, now a disorganized mess, forever setting them down and picking them up, all critical for our departure.

Shortly, the fellow took my papers. This young man was somewhat friendly and spoke a little English. He inspected the car.

I showed him that it was electric. He thought it was cool and five minutes later signed our papers. That was pretty quick and easy. No driver's permit was required in Costa Rica, but the customs agent told us we now needed to get some Costa Rican insurance.

"*Dónde?*" I ask.

He pointed ahead. "Take the first right."

Now that it was time to move on, I couldn't find Dean. He'd slipped away a few minutes earlier to look for a bathroom. I walked across the street and into a small café. Dean was gobbling up a bowl of brown Costa Rican stew, not a very delicious sight. If we didn't have enough problems, he seemed determined to slow us down, bedridden beside a commode for several days. My stomach had been growling, yearning for some real Louisiana gumbo, but the appetite was now gone.

We drove off, but couldn't find the turn for the insurance. Turning around, we got crammed into a gargantuan traffic snarl. There wasn't really a road, just a half-dozen big trucks and as many cars wedged hopelessly in every direction—a mass of mud and mechanization with absolutely no order or rules. Horns and voices echoed off the trees and through the cigarette smoke, exhaust, and gestures.

After acclimating to Central American driving, these traffic jams just become part of the daily routine, something you get numb to, but the scale and mayhem of these debacles is almost indescribable with words. In Dallas or LA, helicopters would be buzzing overhead as hundreds of thousands of Americans looked on in awe at the utter chaos, reverse evolution, civilization breaking down. Somehow, we extricated ourselves in fifteen minutes and made another turn, driving through a large, five-acre, pothole-strewn parking lot hosting more than fifty 18-wheelers. Puttering around, we found two buildings in the back. One of them must be it.

Luckily, the first building I tried was the right one. I presented my papers. The young woman behind the glass started on the lengthy paperwork. This took ten minutes, but she needed a copy of my title and registration. I'd already passed out the two copies I had made. She pointed across the street. I walked over there and got the copies for a dollar, returned and gave her the papers. More stamps.

She handed me the papers and pointed to the other end of the building. "You pay there."

There I went, presenting the papers to another man. I paid the fee for the insurance, about twenty American dollars. Another stamp.

"*No más?*" I ask.

"Good," the man said, waving his finger.

Dean and I returned to the car to drive out of the customs area. We stopped and got out to take a picture in front of the *Bienvenido a Costa Rica* sign. The money changers pestered us, but I didn't bother buying any colones.

As we pulled out of the border crossing, there was one more stop, a guard shed. By now, I was covered in sweat and mentally beat, my mind buzzing. The guard took our paperwork. I held my breath. Did we have everything? He nodded and handed me back the papers. It had taken about three and a half hours to cross the border. Off into the jungle we went.

Highway of Death

Our first sight in Costa Rica was a young man, white, hippie-type, riding a bicycle southbound on the side of the shoulder-less road in ninety-degree temperature. He made us look like we had some sense. There's little to nothing in the border area of northwest Costa Rica, just hills, and thick, verdant vegetation. It was probably twenty miles to the nearest town of any size, and I'm not talking about Peoria—probably something more like a Spanish Tombstone.

Costa Rica, a world away from Nicaragua, is possibly the planet's biggest natural amusement park. A third of the country is preserved, and its biggest industry is tourism, with almost two million visitors a year. Costa Rica only has four and a half million residents. The Ticos, as they call themselves, believe in the *pura vita*, the pure life, and they've had a good run sapping the tree-huggers and weekend adventurers. Walking around some of the ecotourism stops in Costa Rica is like roving the aisles of a Whole Foods in north Dallas.

The country has been peaceful and democratic since it abolished its army in 1948. No wonder the average income and general quality-of-life measurables here are significantly higher than its northern neighbors.

But here on CA-1, in the lightly populated northern border area, we were not on the tourist circuit. A few cows grazed along the road, and occasionally we got a panoramic view of the cloud-covered green volcanoes to the east (plain compared to those of Nicaragua) or the rolling tropical forest.

The traffic was light, and I wanted to speed up, but the speed limits weren't posted. Costa Rican cops have ruined my day more than once over the years. In the old days, all you had to worry about were the local Barney Fifes trying to pick up a little extra cash to take their wives out for a nice dinner, really just lawmen/business-men, but the drug traffickers have of late zeroed in on Costa Rica, and the police presence has increased considerably. Seems like we export a lot of the problems to Central America, be it gangs, CIA-trained death squads, or drug lords trying to get their valuable product to the ready market in middle-class America.

We drove on through the nothing toward Liberia. Every time I sped up, I saw one of the ubiquitous "cow warning" signs that reminded me not to get too gutsy. We crossed a neat old truss bridge on the Rio Liberia and rolled into the town of the same name, a lit-tle oasis in the jungle.

Liberia will give you some sense of the ecotourism craze that has swept through Costa Rica. In 1995, I heard they were upgrad-ing the little airport here for international service. This was the stupidest thing I'd ever heard. Then the town had maybe thirty thousand people. And it was in the middle of nowhere, seventy-five miles down rickety roads to the cloud forest in the Cordillera Tilaran mountains and about the same to a few dusty beach towns on the west coast. Today, Liberia has more than sixty thousand residents, and even in the off-season the airport has sixteen daily flights to the United States and Canada, greeting almost seven hundred thousand travelers annually.

Still, there's not much to see around Liberia, and we drove on. The scenery was sparse, the road slicing through vacant green hills. South of town, the highway was under construction, being widened to four lanes. Thirty more miles to the ranching town of Canas, the only sight the raging Rio Tenorio, now just a boulder-littered rock garden around a trickle of water, but known for its rafting and Class Four rapids in the wet season. The traffic grew steadily, but we averaged 30 mph, the drive pleasant through the incessant, undulating hills.

Dean's mood today was merry. He had borrowed my computer the night before and was again uploading videos and updating his Facebook page.

"What day of the week is it?" I asked.

"Does it matter?"

"I see another Walmart. I'm going to buy a second computer so you can stay happy, and I can get some shit done."

I felt as free as a parakeet, though the construction of the modern highway removed some of the alluring alien experience of the setting, especially since the workers all looked almost identical to the concrete-forming crews along any American highway in the early twenty-first century (and probably spoke the same language). To help ease the grief induced by the beehive of construction and long line of new white concrete, I checked my cell phone to make sure I had no bars.

But everything changed in Canas. Here the road transitioned back to a winding, cascading two-lane asphalt belt, the traffic becoming unimaginably thick.

Before long, we bumped ahead at 20 mph in an endless line of vehicles stretching as far as I could see, which wasn't far. Half the vehicles were 18-wheelers or buses, and the Ticos drove worse than the Guatemalans. The fifty-three miles to Puntarenas took over two and half hours, some of the worst hours of my life.

The big trucks passed each other everywhere. Oncoming, the idiots raced by without a thought and with complete disregard for the terrain. Everyone constantly slammed on their brakes to allow the maniacs to get back in their lanes.

Actually, the cars and trucks hustling around us frightened me more than the oncoming traffic. They whipped out into the opposite lane, barreling around me and forcing the row of vehicles in front of us to make a hole to let them back in.

A few times, I thought I was about to witness a suicide, but at the last moment in the deadly game of "chicken," the trucks parted like the Red Sea and two tractor-trailers blew by each other only inches apart. My breath got heavy, my skin clammy. Were we about to experience a field experiment testing Mr. Newton's laws of motion? We passed one wreck, the three-axle truck literally in the bottom of a small river.

The Tesla's spunk was our only salvation. On several occasions, I passed a line of trucks, not because I was in a hurry, but because everyone around me was so bunched up and changing lanes, the brinkmanship was too much for my nerves. When I could, I puffed a few cigarettes to the filter wondering if Ticos only found out there was a blind spot in their mirrors as they were being whisked into an ambulance.

My concern growing, I almost pulled over several times. After all we'd been through, now I felt like we had the greatest chance to end our trip—and everything else—in an instant. I thanked my lucky stars that the Costa Rican insurance didn't cover Dean to drive. Those complicated border crossings may be a blessing in disguise. With Dean behind the wheel video recording, I would have likely given up cigarettes for whatever they were smoking back at Lake Atitlán in Guatemala.

Dean spent the time on the horrifying highway trying to distract me. As the traffic got very hectic, my hands gripping the wheel, eyes alert for an oncoming madman storming into our lane, he turned on his camera, trying to interview me about the trip. Or worse, cranked up some awful rap music, prompting me to "get down" for the camera while I drove.

Via another long-standing, classic, steel-truss bridge, we motored over the Rio Guacimal and into the outskirts of Puntarenas. To my relief, the traffic slowed to a snail's pace. I'd never been through such a harrowing traffic jam, except for maybe Tapline Road on the Iraq-Saudi Arabia border during the Gulf War. I felt as if I had just survived an armed robbery, the assailant wanting to take only my wallet.

Dean and I deliberated on our destination. It was about four in the afternoon. I guessed we had about seventy-five miles left in the tank. Dean pulled out a few notes on some towns we'd researched the night before. Sixty miles to San José and forty-five to the beach resort of Jaco. We decided to get our toes wet in the surf. I was in no mood for more traffic.

We drove on past Puntarenas, not much of a tourist town, but a pretty nostalgic place. Once known as the Pearl of the Pacific, it was a major port in the last century, moving Costa Rica's coffee off to market. Plenty of Americans pass through the town to catch the ferry to the beach towns on the Nicoya Peninsula, but rarely do they slow down to marvel at the rusting relic of yesteryear, its weathered old piers and docks of a bygone era poking into the sea.

We drove across an old railway, the Puntarenas to San José line, long abandoned. The story of Costa Rica's rails and the American who built them, Minor Cooper Keith, is a dramatic novel unto itself, something similar to the construction of the Panama Canal, completed forty years after Keith began his work.

Hired by the Costa Rican government in 1871 to help transport the country's valuable coffee, Mr. Keith, then famous for pushing rails through the daunting Andes, almost carved the country out of the jungle, a western version of Cecil Rhodes and his founding of South Africa and Zimbabwe with the aid of diamonds.

The thick forest and terrible climate proved much tougher than the steep South American slopes. The first twenty miles of rail claimed Keith's three brothers and four thousand other men. The endeavor almost bankrupted the country, and the Costa Ricans ceded the railroad and 5 percent of the country to Keith if he would finish the job.

Keith did eventually finish the railroad in 1890. It is claimed that several of the bridges on the route were so frightening that on the train's maiden trip, the engineer refused to cross them. Daring the engineer, Keith raised an American flag and crawled onto the engine's front grill.

Keith went on to establish the banana industry in Costa Rica. A merger with his banana interest formed the United Fruit Company, and he was the first vice-president. Considering how many Americans visit Costa Rica every year, I'm amazed that so few people know this story. Though out of print, a great book about Keith and these wild and woolly days, *Keith and Costa Rica* by Watt Stewart, was first published in 1964. Filled with scheming, shames, and kickbacks, it should be made into a movie.

The sun barely hanging over the Pacific, we passed by the Carara Biological Reserve, a bird-watchers' paradise—to my eyes just another thick wall of canopy. I've never been much of a bird-watcher. I could probably be coaxed into a lazy afternoon of bird-watching with Julia Roberts, but not Dean Lewis.

We needed to scoot on. Now at a latitude of less than 10 degrees, twilight shrunk by almost thirty minutes. Darkness approached with less warning.

We drove through Tarcoles and over the river by the same name. The tourists lined the bridge to look out at the huge crocodiles sunning on the banks. We saw one big, fat reptile, but this was not really a sight for me. In the last nine months alone, the Louisiana Department of Wildlife and Fisheries has been out twice to my neighborhood to kill the nuisances, alligators, less than two hundred yards from my front door. Louisiana may be more of a virgin wilderness than some of the tourist spots here.

Gringo to the Rescue

The surfers' paradise of Jaco looked as if it had been slapped together on a whim. Shabby shops sat beside high-rise hotels. Neon lights wedged between hammocks. I whiffed the salty air and background stench. The European and Ivy League versions of Southern gals paraded along Jaco's main strip, the Avenida Pastor Díaz. They looked as if they'd just gotten off the beach in Padre Island or Gulf Shores, many sporting my favorite outfit, short cut-offs and a tight T-shirt.

Of late, drug dealers arrived here, and we were soon pulled over. The friendly cops quickly realized that if we needed detainment, it was in a nuthouse instead of the local pokey.

I hadn't researched any hotels for Jaco. Our travels had devolved to the more regal, golden era of centuries past, a time not just before the internet, but before guidebooks, when travelers simply showed up somewhere and looked for a place to stay.

After several stops, we found no place to charge. We pulled over near the police checkpoint and took off in two directions on foot. I flipped through *Lonely Planet* and asked the police about several hotels. Not finding anything, we drove on to the edge of town, where we found a small hotel with five or six nice rooms. The owner, an elderly Tico named Antonio, sat out front in a lawn chair. We looked at a room with a 240-volt air conditioner and explained our situation.

"*Sí*," the old, sun-bleached man said.

I popped the hood. When he saw the big wires, ol' Antonio got confused and started marching around, mumbling.

I pulled out a thick wad of dollars, flipping through them liberally. Ol' Antonio paced some more, studied the wires, and murmured some garbled Spanish. Five more minutes of dealing transpired with electricity still in doubt.

"We ain't got time for this shit," Dean said. "Let's go. The old man can't make up his mind."

We checked another hotel, owned by a European, but it was full, and two or three more, including the Best Western. My three principles: persistence, doom, and tips paid no dividends.

My emotional rocker reclined to desperation and despair. I wondered if I might find some Prozac locally to add to my pillbox. Peanut M&Ms from the console would have to suffice.

Twilight encasing the town, the car down to thirty miles of battery, we pulled into Morgan's Cove, part casino, part ranch-style beach resort.

I explained our situation to the hotel staff, showing off the car. The hotel's air conditioning was directly wired, but the young woman behind the counter buzzed the manager. As I waited out-side, a taxi delivered an American couple to the hotel. The bell-boy earned his tip, unloading six big bags. Were they moving here? Damn, we gringos have a lot that we think we can't live without.

In a few minutes, the manager appeared out of the night, a big, thick, white guy, late thirties, with a Midwestern accent. Joey Teja hailed from Michigan. Small planet.

He took us to the hotel's laundry room. It had a 240-volt socket, standard NEMA 6-20 that I had a plug for. The voltmeter read no power. We flipped a switch. I removed the socket cover, wiggled a few wires, still no power.

We next entered the hotel's shop, a wooden structure next door, but found no socket. We did find a breaker box with two red leads, 240 volts, terminating into dead-end bolts.

Joey pointed. "There's your 240 volts."

I quickly checked the leads. Hot and 240.

I studied the box from several angles. In Managua, I had watched the hotel electrician wire us up. Now, it was my turn.

I turned to Joey. "Can we cut the power in here?"

Joey turned to the two Costa Rican maintenance men, eyeing the proceedings with interest. He spouted some Spanish.

One of the Ticos disappeared and in a few seconds the lights went out.

I went to the car and got my flashlight, toolbox, and plug bag. With the flashlight, I checked the power. Off. Good.

Then I rigged up the same plug we'd used in Managua and wired it in. It was a little disorienting about which of the two grounds to choose. I guessed, and nodded to the Tico to turn on the power. We all stepped back. The lights came on. Nothing exploded. But I couldn't get the meter to read 240 volts.

The next hour passed, my body perspiring heavily in the muggy air, the light in the shop constantly going off and on as I wired and re-wired, seven or eight different combinations, swapping grounds and plugs, trying to find the right configuration.

My blood pressure skyrocketed, cigarettes were consumed rapidly as the room's lights went on and off, the Ticos mumbling to themselves, everybody wincing at the moment of truth when we flipped the switch back on. I didn't know whether to chuckle or cry at the unfolding farce. Dean shot several good videos of this that later turned into internet sensations, but eventually, around eight, after more than an hour of trial and error wiring, we got a green positive from the Tesla's adapter.

As Dean went to get the car, I stepped out of the shack, the ocean breeze against my sweaty body refreshing. I wiped my fore-head and turned up a bottle of water, gulping down the refresh-ing liquid. Overhead, the big palms swayed. The stars twinkled. To my right, the tourists hanging around the beach laughed as they enjoyed their typical two-week vacation.

After Dean drove over the back lawn to the shop, we set the charging rate to 18 amps and would be fully charged by ten o'clock the next morning. It had been a long, twelve-hour day, and I hadn't even checked in or unpacked, but we'd gone 261 miles, our best day yet.

Thirty minutes later, confident the car was charging, I took a cab to the strip. Jaco was warming up for the night, the swanky bars beginning to fill. Would I ever have loved to roll into one of the social establishments, drop my credit card, down a bottle of rum, and display my Southern charm that had helped get us this far in an attempt to persuade the blue-eyed foreigners to show me their tans up close. But we had a car charging, and I needed supplies and food.

Ducking into a supermarket to buy some water and other essentials, my hair flowed as freely as some of the mellowed-out beach bums. In the rush before departure from the United States, trimming the mop had not been a priority. (I cut my own hair and have for more than a decade.) I didn't have enough money in all my accounts, including retirement, to sway Dean to put scissors to it. Worse, I had run out of hair gel, and with the long days and the open windows, I was starting to look like Shaggy.

I bought some Costa Rican hair product and four bottles of water for ten American dollars, then stepped out of the grocery to solve my other problem. Next door was a Costa Rican pizza house, the enticing smell lingering in my nose. I pulled out my wallet and confidently strolled into the pizza house for the local special.

Touch and Go

I was up early the next morning, five-ish, the night's sleep spotty at best. Three times during the night, I got up to check on the car. Then, with Dean still snoring, I grabbed my laptop. *EV World* ran the story and posted the podcast of our interview. I didn't bother to read the details, but noticed that, in less than a day, the story had been viewed well over a thousand times and had quite a few positive comments. Somebody in the developed world cared about us after all.

Not having time to gloat, I pulled up Google Maps to figure out where we were headed. I did a quick general search of driving in Costa Rica. *Rough Guides* travel books said:

> Ticos frequently risk life and limb passing large trucks on blind curves, but don't be tempted to follow suit— Costa Rica has one of the world's highest road-accident rates.

This was not news. I turned to the bigger problem. We had one last physical obstacle to surmount, the vast, sparsely populated jungle of southern Costa Rica and northern Panama. Though I'd never been to either of these areas, I had heard about the huge, largely empty tropical forest. Adding to my anxiety, I had asked Joey the night before if he knew somewhere to the south where we might get a charge.

His response had been terse and poignant. "There's not much south of Quepos, but the coast road is good, at least in Costa Rica."

Reviewing the maps, trying to gauge the sizes of the towns represented by dots on the map, I found little solace. The guidebook only mentioned five towns in the area with scant recommendations for lodging. I googled "population density North America map." Reviewing one of the maps that popped up, I squinted to study the varying shades of blue. Only the Chihuahua Desert was less populated than the next few hundred miles, and only slightly, but the jungle to the south of us was bigger, at least the portion we had to cross. It would require three days and two charges instead of the two days and one charge we used to cross the Chihuahua Desert.

I settled on David, Panama, as the day's objective, the biggest town in the entire stretch. With about one hundred thousand people, it was 195 miles away. South of David, the guidebook mentioned nothing for 250 more miles.

Dean stirred in bed, stretching his arms, yawning, and looking at me as the morning sun filtered into the room.

I said, "Looks pretty vacant where we're headed. Getting a charge may be touch and go."

Dean rolled back over on his side, turning away from me and the rude sun. "If you haven't noticed, this is touch and go every day!"

I got breakfast and ambled down to the beach. Not much, only a slice of brown, grimy sand. At eight, I made a call to a shipping agent in Panama City. There, the Pan American Highway—and all roads—end at the Darien Gap, a ninety-mile-wide belt of impenetrable jungle and lowland delta. The road picks back up in Colombia on the southern side.

Before the trip I'd done a little research into shipping the car onto Colombia or home from Panama without expending a lot of time or energy, the endeavor too premature. Who knew if and when we'd make it there, or where me might need shipping services? My limited research had told me that shipping the car out of Panama to anywhere would be a time-consuming, bureaucratic nightmare. In any case, we needed a shipper no matter when, where, or if.

I did have a phone number, the local affiliate of the American international shipping company Expeditors. Dean had a friend who worked for the company in Seattle. I quickly realized the shipping problem couldn't be solved over the phone. The language barrier and the oddity of the car and the trip made it too difficult. The English-speaking woman on the end of the line inquired about all kinds of strange things. What was my address in Panama? What type of visa did I have? What was my visa number? Did I have the import paperwork? On what vessel did the car arrive in Panama? This was another obstacle only to be sorted out when we got to it. Like everything else on the trip, we'd figure it out when we got there, wherever *there* was.

By nine-thirty, we said goodbye to Joey and the great staff at Morgan's Cove. On the way out of town, Dean wanted to stop at a store. Inside, I found four cans of smokeless tobacco, Skoal, some type of rare banana-flavored variety. I bought all four. If we got into another Costa Rican traffic mess, I could get my nicotine injection and keep both hands on the wheel, or better yet, triple up, cigarettes, Nicorette gum, and Skoal.

About forty miles south of Jaco, we passed through clean, cute, and laid-back Quepos, wedged snugly between green hills, its colorful two- and three-story hotels and restaurants sitting behind palms and English signs advertising first-world goods and services.

I knew of the town, though I'd never been there. One of the great fishing spots in the world for sailfish and marlin, catch-and-release only, strictly enforced, but also yellowfin tuna, roosterfish, mahimahi, and tarpon. There's also great snorkeling over the coral reefs, rafting the raging Naranjo River, and the nearby popular Manuel Antonio National Park.

The jungle grew more lush and dense, receiving almost two hundred inches of rain a year. For comparison, Hawaii gets the most annual rainfall in the States, about eighty inches, followed by the Gulf Coast at sixty inches.

We drove through the dusty little town of Savegre and over the turbulent river of the same name, now placid in the dry season, but the banks of its deep gorge ripped bare of vegetation and displaying huge wedges of eroded soil that bore tribute to this restless, untamed terrain—when the air fills with energy, and the land and water come alive with the full force of nature.

"Fishing's good here, too," I said. "Freshwater trout. Did you read that weathered sign? Turn right. Organic campground. Whatever the hell that is."

"A gypsy and free-thinkers' nirvana."

"I prefer the hippies that chill out and smoke pot to the in-your-face type."

"Reckon it's a good place to get laid if nothing else, especially in an electric car. Though I wouldn't tell them you're a Republican, fisherman, or that you were in the Army."

"They don't mind the fishing, as long as you only catch what you eat. That's sustainability," I laughed. "But they probably prefer the fish raw."

"I think they eat a lot of berries."

"Maybe it's the new thing. That Costa Rican hair gel I bought was organic."

The out-of-the-way surfing hole of Dominical came and went. Like Quepos, the little beach town appeared to be gearing up for bigger things, like vacant land just on the perimeter of American urban sprawl. Several of its dirt streets were being paved and two hotels were under construction. But this was the end of the gringo track. Few tourists ventured south of Dominical.

Off to our left, the wild Fila Costena Mountains, 5,000 feet high, their summits only fifteen miles away, butted up to the coast. Further afield were the Cordillera de Talamanca Mountains, fifteen miles farther and twice as tall. The mountains swept across the horizon, their jagged ridgelines the deepest green, without a manmade scar. Somewhere over there loomed Cerro Chirripó, one of the tallest mountains in Central America at 12,533 feet.

I felt terrific on the open road, the traffic becoming sparse and heading off to the ends of the earth, the isolated scenery fitting. The entire state of Puntarenas, just a tad smaller than Connecticut, only has about four hundred thousand residents, and only about half of them live south of Jaco in the entire southwestern corner of the country. This is a solitary land, still ruled by a way of life not much different from a century ago. It's what's left of the Costa Rica before the arrival of urban gringos.

Under the soaring trees, we passed through several lazy villages, the side streets unpaved and ringed with simple buildings constructed of rough-cut timber that gave a sense to the wild, pristine setting. The road sliced near the coast. The green hills bumped into the blue sky. Timeless waves crashed into the brown beach. I felt the cheery sun and cool, salty wind on my face, tropical and relaxing.

Was this even reality, or one of those deep dreams we don't know is a dream until we're shaken back to consciousness? In the States, I never drive relaxed like this; I'm always more worried about how fast I can get there as opposed to whether I'll get there. There was nothing to hurry for here.

What would I be doing at home right now if we weren't rolling along in this otherworldly place? Rushing to a meeting? Worried that the battery on my overworked cell phone was too low to return a list of urgent calls and emails? Or banging on the steering wheel because somebody in front wouldn't step on it and get out of the way? The trip had induced a magical state. Too old for college pranks, too young not to give a damn, this was spring break for forty-somethings.

Outside of Puerto Cortés, we bisected miles of banana and African palm groves introduced here a generation ago by United Fruit. The scheming white men from the north left their permanent mark on the land.

I knew a little about Cortés, professionally. The port city of five thousand on the banks of the Rio Terraba also called Rio Diquís, the latter meaning "big water," was considering relocating to higher ground. The tropical storms belting the river and its steep, unique watershed in the nearby mountains produces some of the fastest rising and most tempestuous waters in the world, incessantly flooding the town.

The pace slowed briefly in the cities of Palmar Norte and Palmar Sur, a regional administrative hub where we got back on the Pan American Highway, weaving around a few tricycles laden with goods. In the small traffic snarl, the Ticos smiled and waved as we crossed the infamous Rio Terraba on an old three-span truss bridge, an omnipresent reminder of man's unending struggle with nature on the Ring of Fire. Whoever designed the bridge knew what they were doing.

From here, it was only an hour's drive to hopefully our last overland Central American border crossing. Looking forward to that is like sitting in the dentist's office waiting to have a tooth pulled. But ahead lay a few more wild rivers, Esquinas and Piedras Blancas, and a few jaguars, pumas, and the venomous fer-de-lance viper.

Costa Rica plans to open its third international airport here in the near future. The sands of time here will soon fall faster through the glass. If I ever came back to this land of foaming, powerful rivers and secluded beaches, it might look more like Cape Cod than the almost virgin, wild paradise we saw today.

Redneck Engineering

The border crossing into Panama was standard. No signs, a few tourists, government employees bickering, stamps banging, papers ruffling. All made more complicated and time consuming because the copy machine at Morgan's Cove had not been working and I had to get copies of everything made at the crossing. The hawkers were there on the Panamanian side, but not as fierce as previously. They followed us everywhere, constantly reaching for our passports.

The big problem here was that Dean and I were forced to go through two different areas, I with the car through one processing center, and he, as only a passenger, through another. The complications arose when he didn't have a bus ticket. You can't enter Panama without documented transportation onward. It was always something. Dean's exchange with the immigration officer didn't go well.

I finally paid a hawker to figure it out. The twenty-five dollars was ten more than we'd agreed, but at the moment of truth, our papers dangling in front of us, he upped the ante. It took over two hours, including a dollar for fumigation and fifteen more for Panamanian car insurance.

Pulling out of the border crossing, I slid three fingers of banana Skoal against my bottom lip.

Dean made an ugly face. "You've got a lot of vices, you know that?"

"I've quit one—sex."

"At least we agree on something."

"You've got vices too. You've liberally sampled every local beer for three thousand miles."

"After ten hours in the car with you, I need it. . . and I didn't drink any beer in El Salvador!"

David was only thirty miles on the other side of the border. Panama is the richest country in Central America, English more prevalent here than anywhere else. This should be a breeze. I'd been to Panama before—that is, I'd been to the Canal Zone before.

Panama has about three and a half million people, roughly like Connecticut, but it's five and a half times bigger. Half the country lives in the Canal Zone, only about two percent of the area. Outside of the Canal Zone exists an entirely different, extremely rural Panama.

We drove over the Rio Chico, which experiences the fifth-highest flow velocity in the world. Three years earlier, the torrent of water had collapsed one of the bridge's spans. Thankfully, we traveled during the dry season. In this area, the Pan American Highway is all that traverses the country. A bridge failure here would likely mean a days-long detour over dilapidated, mountain dirt roads. I'd experienced the ordeal before in Central America. It's not pleasurable. You don't go around the bridge—you go around the river.

We rolled into the provincial, slow-moving town of David, a onetime faraway garrison of the Spanish Empire. The remote oasis had little colonial charm left, the town built on a square grid, the architecture functional but uninspiring. The city felt like a frontier town on the American plains filled with bumper-to-bumper traffic and the ever-present honking.

The possibility for ample accommodations and a good charge looked bleak. We had over 90 miles of battery remaining, but nowhere to go. In the 274-mile stretch of road between here and Panama City, our 768-page *Lonely Planet* guidebook for Central America did not mention a single town along the Pan American Highway.

We made two or three passes through town, and finally, around four, pulled into the nicest hotel we saw, the Gran Hotel in the *centro*. I went in. Neither of the two men at the front desk spoke English, but I led them outside for the game of show and tell.

A bilingual guest stopped to look at the car and asked a few questions. He explained our problem to the hotel staff. The undercurrent of concern on the natives' faces spoke volumes.

Soon the hotel manager arrived on the scene. More Spanish followed, the rapid version. I lost all ability to translate. They pointed, nodded, scratched their ears. One of the men got on his radio, and the manager motioned for us to follow him to the side of the building. There, he poked his head into a room under construction.

On the wall below the window was a big socket. I grabbed my voltmeter. Inside I went, to discover the valuable power source—240 volts. Dean quickly grabbed the car's charging adapter, and I my plug bag. Through the heavy fragrance of palms and bananas, I quickly rigged up a plug, but got no green light. Two more attempts failed.

The Tesla's adapter has a four-pole (four-prong) 240-volt plug with two hot wires, a ground wire, and a neutral wire. We hadn't seen a four-prong plug since Texas. The problem with wiring a four-pole plug to a three-pole plug is that some plugs have two hot wires and a neutral, others have two hot wires and a ground.

Which was which was always the question. Before the trip, I had the plugs and adapters systematically arranged and prepped, but after seven countries of scalping together makeshift plugs, my once-organized bag was now only a bag full of random plug parts, loose wires, screws, and plastic covers.

In the States, the different wires have a designated color. That's rarely the case here. It's a never-ending guessing game with Ben Franklin and Thomas Edison's potent force, Latin Russian Roulette. And when you're playing the game, never get too hasty. Always make sure your leads have good connectivity and that there are no cross-overs. Triple-check there are no exposed wires in the plug where you'll be handling it when you finish all this redneck engineering. I had found in recent days that my heartbeat jumped just touching the prongs of my voltmeter to 240-volt leads or sockets. This was precise wiring. A contractor might get his welder fired up without everything perfect, but the Tesla was much more finicky.

As the manager stepped away, Dean took interest in the wiring. "You going to get this worked out, or am I going to have to navigate and take over the wiring?"

I fumbled with the hopeless wires. "In the States, there's no telling how many laws I'm violating, rigging this jumble of shit up. This is strictly off limits for novices. I need to get out of the heat, get my charts, and start over."

We checked into a room above the car, and I went upstairs to sort it all out. I'd prepared some plug charts before the trip for every combination I could imagine. Starting from scratch, I carefully put together a plug for the adapter and socket.

Back downstairs I went, and the Tesla was soon charging at 240 volts and a modest 13 amps. I inspected the charging operation. The Gran Hotel didn't have secure parking. One of my biggest fears on the trip had been the one piece of equipment where there was no redundancy, the Tesla's charging adapter. I had considered buying a backup, but the price was north of 1,000 dollars and delivery time not adequate for our spontaneous departure. If somebody stole the adapter, the trip would be over.

The price of copper has skyrocketed, and even in affluent, suburban America, available copper was quickly pocketed. This year, in tiny Monroe, Louisiana, I had all the copper stolen from three air conditioners at an office I own a stake in. The thieves had taken the time to dissemble the units and strip out the valuable loot right beside a private Catholic school for the town's well-to-do kids. Here, all the prize required was a rapid unplugging.

I pulled out my second backyard engineering marvel. It had gotten us this far. The fifteen-foot, three-eighths-inch cable had meshed, banded eyes on each end. I looped it through one of the car's wheel rims, and with two locks, secured it to each end of the adapter. The adapter could still be stolen, but only with some effort, and I always augmented my masterpiece with a teaser, connecting it to one of our long, 50-amp extension cords. With more than thirty pounds of copper, these were twenty times more valuable than the adapter on the underground market, and I could buy the materials to re-fabricate them at any Central American hardware store. I never secured the extension cords.

Only a fool, even for a thief, would mess around trying to cut the cable holding the adapter to the car when a much grander treasure lay beside it, begging to be stolen.

I stepped back to admire all my handiwork—the fabricated plug leading from the hotel room window and my foolproof security contraption. I even went a little further, a first for the trip. I moved the adapter's green sensor-light over to an area where I could see it flashing from our second-story room. I wouldn't have to get up all night and come outside to make sure we were charging.

My work of art complete, I needed to make a call. I'd gotten an urgent work-related email that morning. Knowing how many trivial things I was daily required to approve, I had ordered a blue signature stamp before I departed. But only I could answer this inquiry, a question about some specifications I'd written on a levee-repair project.

This was a reminder that everything around me was only a temporary interlude from the cumbersome world that awaited me in the near future. And focusing on engineering specifications brought it back all too quickly.

• • •

After I graduated from LSU, I was sent off to the intoxicating town—oops—village of Amelia, Louisiana, population 2,459. That was my bonus for all those years in college. I'd really only gone to graduate school to extend my time partying and chasing girls, and only selected engineering because my major professor had coaxed NASA into paying the bills (which makes you wonder what else our government wastes money on). It wasn't exactly a free ride. I did have to maintain the minimally acceptable GPA in classes filled with whiz kids setting the curve.

For surviving this, I was rewarded with a job writing project specifications for new offshore oil and gas platforms. A few months after my arrival in Amelia, I was offshore working when my boss came out for a couple of days to look around.

One afternoon, he said, "Randy, I want to go take a nap. Give me that book of specifications."

I handed him the two hundred or so bound pages of technical jargon I had slaved over for months.

He scanned the cover page. "Nothing puts me to sleep faster than reading this shit."

• • •

The burdensome phone call over, I went upstairs. Amazingly, Dean had not yet confiscated my computer. Checking my inbox, I had more than a dozen emails about the trip, many from unknown senders. Some of the emails congratulated us. Others asked for pictures, information, videos.

I checked *EV World*'s web page. The article now had thousands of views and a bunch of comments. I did a quick Google search. Antony Ingram had done a story on the trip for *Green Car Reports*, another industry webpage, and Yahoo, the *Christian Science Monitor*, and several outlets had picked up his story. One of the comments was completely pleasing.

> Leave it to some guys from Louisiana to come up with something as dangerous as this.

I briefly searched the Tesla Motors and Tesla Motors Club message boards. Already several pages of posts were up. A few comments on the first page:

- Panama run—most daring road trip yet?
- It seems some owners from Louisiana decided to drive to Panama. Yes, the country.
- That is probably the boldest trip yet.
- Wow, this is a crazy drive! They've already reached Jaco, Costa Rica. They report to be tying directly into 240v lines (i.e., no plugs!). This trip makes driving from LA to NYC look like a walk in the park.
- That is crazy cool!

- Yowza. This is making our drive to Alaska seem like a walk through a substation!
- Wow, just wow. Some big cojones there.

To say that this brought a smile to my face or filled my soul with utter bliss would be an understatement, but I was beat tired. We hadn't had a day off since the mountain village of Comitán in Mexico, all the days ten to twelve hours on the road with never a break or even a stop for lunch, then the very taxing charging, planning, etc. There were no weekends on this trip.

I still needed to see where we might go tomorrow. Nothing lay ahead for almost three hundred miles. We needed one more charge to make it to Panama City. Surely, we could find something in Panama's northern bush?

The Real Jungle

By ten-fifteen the next morning, we had 233 miles in the tank and stormed into the green wall of vegetation to see what we might find, ready for the challenge. I'd fallen asleep the night before at eight-thirty. I never do that. It was me instead of the car that needed charging. I wasn't sure how I got to sleep because Dean persuaded a poor local trumpeter, outside the window, to serenade us for much of the night.

· · ·

The citizens of David had been kind and helpful. Panama is the one country in Central America where the residents should like Americans, the one place where our meddling, at least in my opinion, has been to their benefit.

We created the country. Teddy Roosevelt stole the almost-empty jungle from Colombia to set up the little puppet state. We then built the country's extensive infrastructure, including the great canal. Mr. Roosevelt was certainly a man of action, summing up the entire process in a sentence:

I took the Canal Zone and let Congress debate, and while

the debate goes on, the canal does also.

Decades later, we gave it all to the Panamanians free of charge. In 1989, we invaded to remove Manuel Noriega, the country's military dictator. Mr. Noriega had been helpful subduing the Red Menace, but after we licked the Commies the United States government finally decided it was time to quit overlooking his drug trafficking and abysmal human rights record. There have been a few small issues over the decades, but America's presence here in the Canal Zone, an American Territory for seventy-six years, has meant general peace and stability for the country for over a hundred years.

· · ·

A few hours into the drive, we'd seen nothing but green hills, the landscape the most rural of the entire trip, along the base of the five thousand-foot Serranía de Tabasará Mountains. In three hours on the road, all we saw were two gas stations and a three-structure settlement. More disconcerting, for most of the drive, I saw no power poles along the road, a first for the trip over such a long stretch.

The road was okay, your standard potholes, one every mile or so that could ruin your day, but we stumbled onto a long, raggedy patch of concrete filled with jagged, sharp edges where the surface had buckled or failed. The worst stretch of paved road we'd yet crossed. I kept waiting for a tire to pop, if not two. The Goodyears passed the test, rolling over the vile concrete as I held my breath.

I turned to Dean. "Go, Goodyear, go!"

"Your elitist heart is going to be broken when you find out they were made in China or Malaysia."

"We ain't home yet. This is a lost world."

"Yeah, I think we finally found the *real* jungle."

We were forced through two police checkpoints, the officials displaying the Latin courteousness and happiness we need more of in the States. At one, we went through the "show and tell" again, the entire security staff at the isolated post requiring pictures with us and the car before we were allowed to depart.

The sights were minimal. I did see a few big, round birds, brightly-colored like a rainbow, and sporting long beaks. Macaws? Toucans? Despite constant scanning, to my disappointment, I saw none of the sloths that populate the region. They're hard to see. Clinging to the thick tree canopy, the chubby creature's only defensive mechanism is its stealth and slow locomotion.

We did pass right by the Barro Blanco Hydroelectric Dam, under construction, the white concrete monolith climbing up out of the jungle right beside the road. If not for the slim power in our batteries, I would have stopped to gawk. We rarely get to see something like this in the Western Hemisphere these days, man conquering nature so brazenly and in such a rural, inhospitable setting. I'm currently an engineer on the largest dam built in Louisiana in several decades, but it's small potatoes compared to this. The two hundred-foot-tall concrete structure rose above the green canopy, announcing a better world for everything.

To say the dam has incited controversy, locally and worldwide, would be a massive understatement. Protesters have blocked the Pan American Highway for days (we don't need that now), and even in the last year, locals have been murdered by cloaked assailants.

Two outside, independent authorities were brought in to analyze the situation, world-renowned experts with no skin in the game. Their conclusion: no environmental impact, but significant harm to the local residents. The controversy has taken the focus away from its proper target: providing adequate compensation for the people impacted.

An important point in the environmental debate is often over-looked. The wealthier a society is, the cleaner the air and water—and a longer and happier life for little Kristi or Gabriela (or baby panda, for that matter). We dominated the American West, over-powered it, damming every river, pushing a rail or highway across every pass, populating every scenic valley. Today, the air and water in most of the American West is some of the cleanest in the world, the residents no longer worried about how they are going to eat, but how they'll get their kids into a better school.

So here in this jungle, the people may decide that inundat-ing some villages is a good trade-off for being able to have their children born in a modern, clean, electric-powered hospital, or building a new sewer and water plant that would benefit the whole community. They should have the right to make that choice.

Meanwhile, back at mile 120, we pulled into the one of two possible charging points, Santiago District. I didn't see much, a few hotels, minimal standards. We might get a charge, might not.

With almost 140 miles of battery left, we decided to push on to Penonomé, a little bigger and 60 miles on. Two hours later we rolled into town, stopping at a nice hotel on the city's edge.

I was promptly told that no 240- or 120-volt power was for sale, rent, or use. We found two other hotels, one decrepit, but the other with window units. The rooms were all on the second floor, but the ACs had 240-volt sockets I could use. I explained every-thing. We could run the cord out of the room's window and park on the street. Ten minutes of begging and pleading, waiting to see the owner. They didn't like the idea. The more I implored, the more unwavering they got.

We checked the GPS and maps. It was only ninety-four miles to Panama City. We had about eighty miles of battery. We might make it if we drove slow enough, but that was cutting it too close, especially with what we'd seen that morning, but a good 120-volt charge would get us there. It was about three. If we could get plugged in by four, we could add about thirty or forty miles to our batteries by daylight.

I went back to the first hotel. Inside, I tried again, sweet-talking the cute Panamanian manager. Doom was the theme. She needed to pitch in, or else. "I just need a standard, two-prong plug." I pointed to a lamp, walked to it, and put my hand on the socket. "I'll buy two rooms and pay for the electricity."

She sought the assistant manager's eye, conversed in Spanish, and then called the owner. Shortly the hotel electrician arrived.

"Okay," the manager said. "But you can't plug into the hotel. Pablo will make a plug in the parking lot."

Outside we went. I watched as Pablo rigged up a 120-volt plug at the base of a light pole, but his antiquated old voltmeter, only a needle gauge and two wires, their ends stripped bare, read no power. Pablo's eyes got big when I pulled out my bright yellow, digital Fluke voltmeter. He looked at it as if it was some type of space machine from the future, but it too said no power.

I showed Pablo my fifty-foot, 120-volt extension cord. Even in the States, I have trouble getting the Tesla's adapter to go green with 120-volt power and cords longer than this—there's just not enough juice. We stretched the cord out to a maintenance room beside the hotel and got it plugged in with a few feet to spare.

Checking the car's charging gauge, we were powering up, but minimally. We'd make it to Panama City with twenty-five or thirty miles to spare!

I turned to the manager, smiling. "I'll take a room."

She smiled back. "Two rooms."

Possibly we've been too adamant about this capitalism thing to our southern friends.

We checked in. I scanned my inbox, again full of strange emails. One came from my fiction editor in New York. The subject line read: "What the . . .?"

I did a little googling. The EV blogosphere in the United States was now filled with the news and stories of the two "coon asses" who were almost to Panama in an electric car. I emailed Bill, Marcus, and Mike Dunckley the good news. We'd make it into Panama City, the end of the road, tomorrow. I'd send some good pictures of the car at the canal.

Saved by the Marriott—Again

I looked up at the pre-dawn sky. Without the contamination of city lights, the stars shone gloriously. The night sky had changed considerably over the past few weeks. Overhead, Orion sparkled, the mythical Greek hunter's belt now almost directly overhead. To the north, I barely saw Ursa Minor, hovering over the horizon. I couldn't even see the North Star, probably hidden behind some trees. Here, it would be rather easy to calculate our latitude of only eight and a half degrees. How much fun the calculation might be if I had my sextant or even a protractor and could find the horizon. Am I a dork?

Anxiously, I looked to the east, waiting for the crimson glow of twilight. The internet at the hotel was good, and I'd spent much of the night answering requests from the States for information about our trip, some in the press. I'd typed out a one-page summary and sent it off to several people, and also uploaded a half-dozen of Dean's videos and fifty or so pictures to a file-sharing site.

After several requests, Dean also made his Facebook page public.

Somewhere in the last three thousand miles, I'd lost the newer of my two pairs of glasses, the older pair requiring more squinting as I uploaded the data. Along the way, I'd accidentally reset the Tesla's trip meter that not only logs miles traveled, but more importantly, total kilowatt-hours used. The data was lost to history, the latter possibly of some scientific value, a real-world field test of the car's energy consumption over third-world terrain.

My best calculation was that we'd driven about three thousand direct road miles, but that didn't include all the side trips to get a charge (some of these significant), wrong turns, etc. We were likely well over the three-thousand-mile mark. And we had only ninety-four to go.

The EV blogosphere was still fluid with inquiries about who these madmen were who managed to get a Tesla charged every day against such a daunting third-world backdrop. People were even researching me, posting my education and professional credentials. Beside the hotel's front desk, I found a set of scales. Wow—I'd lost nine pounds. Could this be an annual event to relieve me of loathsome exercise?

The night before, I'd booked us into the Panama City Marriott. Why not? The Marriott has thus far been good to us. This was a first for the trip, actually knowing where we were going, and getting a reservation. I hoped it wasn't premature, or a bad omen.

The eastern sky turning rosy, we packed up and pulled out of Penonomé with 128 miles of battery to go the 94 miles. In the calm of morning, I couldn't help but think that the world was watching, at least a lot of the electric-car world anyway. A single thought rammed into my brain. Do not have a wreck! Do not screw this up—especially now.

I had my work cut out. This morning, we drove almost directly east, into the rising sun. And as morning traffic increased, it didn't take long to realize that Panamanian drivers suffer from the same Central American affliction as everybody else. They're in a hurry to transfer their wealth, minus the cost of the undertaker, to their families.

We drove through the Scarlet Martinez International Airport, right under the middle of the runway via a new tunnel opened only three months earlier. Before that, the Pan American Highway actually crossed the tarmac! I was a little disappointed that the new tunnel was open. We had dodged everything else on the trip. Looking out for a landing Airbus would have been only too fitting.

The airport, once the Río Hato Army Air Base, was one of the focal points of the American invasion in 1989. In the first action of the conflict, the Air Force bombed the base, followed by a dramatic air assault on the airport by the US Army Rangers, who parachuted in. A battle ensued, but by morning, the Rangers had prevailed, capturing the airfield and 250 prisoners.

By nine, we were stuck in traffic in the Panama City suburb of Balboa. Dean tried to find the Marriott with the GPS without luck. We tried to plug in the address, but that too was hopeless, hitting another snag often encountered while traveling in Central America. Places rarely have addresses. Occasionally, something out on a solitary road will have a conventional street address with a number and road name, but that's the exception. Typically, addresses only give a general intersection of two major roads. Here's the address for the Panama Marriott:

52nd St. and Ricardo Arias
Av. Ricardo Arango
Ciudad de Panamá, Panamá 832-0498

The GPS had no clue what that meant. I make maps, and had a map in front of me, and I didn't know what it meant. I went out of my way later to have this translated. It means the Marriot is on either 52

St. or Ricardo Arias. That's just one street, but somewhere around the Marriott, around Avenue Ricardo Arango, it changes names. In American lingo, find where 52 St. changes to Ricardo Arias. That should be near Avenue Ricardo Arango. Then look around. The Marriott will be close. Close is open to interpretation also.

Now a veteran of Central American navigation, I did make it a point while booking the room to study some pictures of the hotel so I knew what it looked like—in this case, a long, thin, fifteen-story building with an art-deco façade, topped with a big, red Marriot sign.

Correlating the map and GPS, we did find a park within a mile of the Marriott and punched it in. At a terribly slow pace, we crossed the Bridge of the Americas. The one thousand-foot steel arch rose four hundred feet above Panama Bay.

To the left, we spied the one hundred-year-old Mira Flores Locks on the Panama Canal. The wonder of the world, a grid of concrete cutting the green backdrop, it looked like a model toy from the bridge. To the right, dozens of ships sat patiently in the bay waiting their turn in the shimmering, immense blue water. Ahead, the modern, shining skyscrapers of Panama City, the closest thing we'd seen to a modern metropolis since Houston, rose from the sea to the heavens.

I'm not sure the GPS even knew we were in Panama City. We took three or four wrong turns, but eventually found ourselves on the Avenida Balboa that runs north along the Pacific. We drove right by the statue of Vasco Nuñez de Balboa, still staring out over the Pacific five hundred years after he crossed the Isthmus of Panama to be the first European to look west and see the blue waters.

We took a few more wrong turns in the web of one-way streets and taxis. I'd never seen so many taxis, 80 percent of the vehicles. The little yellow machines scurried everywhere, adding to the anarchy. Panama City was not laid out on a planned, symmetrical grid like Manhattan. It was more like some scaled-up parish seat in Louisiana, built around snaking bayous. Two steps forward, one back, we continued like a headless chicken another ten minutes before we saw the Marriott, poking up through the tendrils of skyscrapers. We made a few more trips around the neighborhood, the building getting no closer. It actually seemed to get smaller.

I saw the Crowne Plaza, pulled in, and got some directions from the bellboy. As he talked, I presented a piece of paper, the most reliable means of getting directions south of the Rio Grande, and made a scribbling motion. "*Mapa.*"

Only one more wrong turn and we pulled into the Marriot, with twenty-four miles left in the tank. I checked us in and explained our situation. Soon, I was downstairs in the underground parking lot. The Marriot had a three-prong, NEMA 10-30, 30-amp socket, exactly like the one for my drier in Louisiana that I often use to charge the car. The socket sat right beside a parking spot, no extension cord required.

A few tips later, one of the hotel's vans was moved, and we were charging at 22 amps. I reached in the car's console and pulled out the address of the shipping company.

One of the bellboys pointed. "Down the hill. Take left on 52. One kilometer."

Grabbing the paperwork, off I went. Thirty minutes later I still hadn't found the shipping agent's office. Now perspiring in something akin to a Louisiana summer, I studied the map and asked for directions, but in fifteen more minutes still hadn't found the office. I employed an old tactic, tested true all over the world. I waved down a cab, hopped in, and handed the driver the address.

We made a few rights, then lefts, through two traffic circles. Five minutes later, he pulled over and pointed to a building.

Inside, I found only a bank. Fifteen minutes of walking and asking put me back at my original location. I went into two offices, questioning and again asking. In a travel agency, an elderly lady finally drew me a map. Behind a building, I walked through a gate, around a corner, up an elevator. An hour and a half after leaving the Marriot, my clothes now soaked, I entered the shipping company's office.

One young woman spoke terrific English. She was a blonde with an accent that sounded like she was from Lima, Ohio. I couldn't believe it when she informed me she was from Uruguay. After a little back and forth, she finally understood my problem.

"I'll be right back," she said, walking off. "I'll talk to the manager."

Five minutes later she returned. "We don't do this." She handed me a piece of paper. "But here is someone who specializes in this."

I looked at the card.

Mario Alvarado
Metropolitan Movers
507-392-2731
Panamá, Rep. de Panamá

I dialed the number.

Mario answered, his English good, but not great.

I explained the situation.

"Yes, yes, I do that all the time," he said. "Please come by and see me next week."

Next week? "No, No," I said. "I need to see you today."

"Let me give you my address."

Fear filled my mind. No way I would find anything here. "No, I am at the Marriot. You know it?"

"Yes, in town?"

"Yes. Can you come by today? I have the car. You can look at it." I looked at my watch. "At three o'clock."

"Okay."

"Call this number when you get there. I will come down and meet you in the lobby."

An hour later I sat in the lobby awaiting the call. Before the trip, we'd planned to drive on to South America. How far, I didn't know. Only the northern countries in South America—Colombia, Ecuador, and Peru—have the same power grid as the States, but I'd heard that shipping a non-Panamanian car to any of these three was very difficult.

In my mind, we'd done enough, but if we could find a quick ferry or ride around the Darien Gap, I was open to going on, especially since the world had not ended when I left the States. Somehow, it appeared that everybody and everything back home still managed to operate smoothly in my absence.

Almost on time, my phone rang. I found Mario in the lobby, and we sat down at a table. I presented all my papers.

Of mixed descent with common black hair and big brown eyes, he was taller than most Panamanians. Dressed in casual slacks and a cotton shirt, he looked educated and professional as he studied the papers for a few minutes.

"How about shipping the car to Colombia or Ecuador?" I asked, sipping some bottled water.

Still flipping through the papers, he groaned. "This is very difficult—but it is possible."

"How about shipping to the States?"

"This is much easier. No problem."

"How long will that take?"

Mario looked over the papers. "You have all the paperwork, including this. Very important." He held up one of the papers I'd paid the border hawker twenty-five dollars for (he may have actually been a good little businessman instead of a crook). "I have very good relationship with Panamanian customs. Everything is smooth. I cannot make any guarantees, but we may be able to have the car picked up here in ten days." He put his pen to his chin. "Where do you want the car shipped?"

"Houston."

"Okay, no problem. Then another ten days to two weeks to get it to Houston. This is all contingent on the shipping schedule and availability, of course. I have no control over that."

I leaned back in my chair. I wanted to smoke the last of my Central American cigarettes. Twenty to twenty-five days! And this was optimistic. If shipping to America was "easy," South America was out of the question. Two weeks to pick up the car? Where would I keep it for two weeks? Would I be here another month? All kinds of terrible scenarios rushed through my mind.

"I will prepare an estimate for you," Mario said, holding up the papers. "Can I have these?"

"Yes." I nodded. "They are copies."

"I will get you the estimate first thing Monday morning."

Monday morning. What day of the week was it? I looked at my phone. It was Friday afternoon. "I need the estimate and details today or tomorrow."

Mario smiled. "It is the weekend, but my company has expedited service, seven days a week. There is a small fee, of course, but I can have you something tomorrow."

I scratched out my email address on a piece of paper. "Yes, please. Email is the best way to get me, or my phone. Please email me today or tomorrow." I stood up, extended a hand in a terminal gesture. "One other question. Can you store the car? I don't have anywhere to keep it."

Mario put the papers in his briefcase, then stood. "I will talk to you tomorrow. No, we don't usually store cars. We only come get them once customs is ready. I will check and see if I might find somewhere to store the car."

Shipping turned out to be much more complicated than I ever expected. A little internet research turned up Mario's company's web page. It looked formal and legit, but was in Spanish. I did notice a few logos of Western clients on the page.

The bigger problem was the time. In a perfect world, I would have loved to stay in Panama for a few more weeks, possibly on the beach drinking rum, flirting with the local girls, writing this book, and then drive on south, our dreamlike break from the world going on and on. But I lived in the real world. If we were going to be away another month, it needed to be driving.

I looked over my shoulder to Dean, lounging on the couch and watching TV. I knew he wanted to push on. Always had, but he didn't have a job or the title to the car in his name. "South America is out. It's too much trouble, and more importantly, will take too long. Mario said it may be three to four weeks just to get the car to Houston. Looks like we'll be headed home in a few days."

Dean moaned and groaned. "You're making a mistake. One you will one day regret."

I turned back to the computer and typed out an email to Bill, Marcus, and Mike.

Hey guys: we made it. We'll likely be home in few days

with the car to follow in a few weeks. We will try to get
some good pictures around the canal tomorrow. Best,
and thanks for everything, Randy

I had a bigger problem. Where would I keep the car for several
weeks? I went downstairs to the front desk and asked to see the manager. She wasn't in, but the assistant manager, a middle-aged lady
who spoke excellent English, came out of her office to greet me.

I explained the situation. "Would it be possible for me to keep
the car here for a couple of weeks until the shipping agent has everything worked out? He can then come here and get it. If there's a
fee for parking, I'll gladly pay it."

When we'd checked in earlier that day, I'd told the assistant
manager our story, and that several media outlets in the States were
covering us.

She produced a big smile, apparently having done some
internet surfing to confirm my crazy story. "I have been checking
on you, Mr. Denmon. I didn't know you and your friend were so
famous." She motioned to the front door and the head bellboy, a
tall, slender Panamanian named José, stepped into the lobby.

The two commenced another one of those frustrating Spanish
conversations, the words far too fast for me to comprehend.

The assistant manager then flashed her eyes at me. "This will
be no problem. I just need you to write me a letter explaining all
this to me, and stating the Marriott will not be responsible for the
car. Do not worry, the car is in good hands, very safe, but I have
to have the letter for my bosses. You understand. But we would be
glad to keep your car."

"*Muchas, muchas gracias.*" The Marriot to the rescue again!

Sometimes You Just Have to Wing It

Dean and I stood in the portico of the Marriott looking out into the mid-morning Panamanian traffic disaster.

I scratched my chin. "I booked us on the midday flight to Houston tomorrow."

"I hope you didn't sit us together," Dean moaned. "I've had enough of your ass for a while."

"Don't worry." I laughed. "We're on opposite ends of the plane."

The Tesla now refilled with kilowatts, we hoped to tour the city, the canal, and hopefully take some great pictures with the car. There wasn't a whole lot to do in Panama City, especially before dark, but we had some rare time to kill.

As I waited on the staff to bring the car around, (part of my ingratiation with the hotel staff upon our arrival had been letting them drive the car around the block to the hotel's parking area), I looked at the casino attached to the hotel, one of many that filled the city. The suckers streamed into the money machine. The casinos reminded me that I hadn't engaged in one of my favorite pastimes since before Christmas, gambling. I'm no junkie, and I steer away from the state-backed rackets—lotteries and casinos. I do have a degree in mathematics, after all. But I'm not afraid to let it ride on a horse race, card game, football game, or friendly golf match. I mean, after all, I am a red-blooded American. We need some vices other than nicotine and booze to get through the week.

The night before, I bought some new clothes. The four changes that accompanied me across the border needed more than a hotel wash. Now adorned in a new shirt and my only pair of clean jeans, we stormed into the chaos of Panama City.

I'd been here before, but couldn't believe the city's growth, metamorphosis even. Was it really a decade since I'd been here? The years all now merge and pass so fast I really had no idea.

New, glass high-rises pierced the sky everywhere, the construction crane seemingly the city bird. Panama City resembled a slightly smaller version of some of the world's other major port cities, Hong Kong or Singapore. The last time I was here, the Hard Rock Café was the biggest Western attraction in town. Now, dozens of hip and snazzy restaurants and bars lined the streets.

Spurred on by its banking industry and the growth in the worldwide import/export industry spawned from the West's insatiable consumerism and never-ending demand for more stuff at lower prices, the Panamanian economy, fueled by the canal, is now growing at about nine percent a year, one of the highest in the world, and well in excess of America's measly 2 percent annual growth rate.

I'm not sure who these Panamanians are—a true melting pot of the Western Hemisphere. Like most of Latin America, they're more brown than white or black. Almost nobody was here before the canal. The US government's census of the Canal Zone a hundred years ago put the population at fifty thousand, and at that point the canal project was well into its fifth year. I think most everybody, or their parents or grandparents, have simply immigrated here in the last generation or two.

We passed by a neighborhood populated with big, ostentatious residences announcing the country's newfound wealth. The Panamanians have invented one of the most humorous and unique names for these local showoffs, *rabi-blancos*. English translation: white-butts. I chuckle every time I hear it.

We headed for the Mira Flores locks right outside of town to see the engineering marvel and hopefully get some cool pictures of it and the car.

Whirling through the congested, roundabout streets, I picked Dean's brain. "Seems a little reckless to just leave an eighty thousand-dollar car with a stranger in Central America, especially one that's in such demand in the States. But I need to confirm with Mario—or not—today. What do you think?"

"Did you check him out? Search online to see if anybody has complained about him?"

"A little. Didn't find much. On a deal like this, I guess you've just got to wing it. That's how we got here. Not much else you can do. I'm not going to hang around for a month. The hotel clerk told me there are some good bars and restaurants on the Calle Uruguay, right around the corner. Be nice to down some rum and not have to worry about the car or getting up. I may smoke one of those Panamanian cigars tonight. You game?"

"Hell, yeah. If we can find our way back to the hotel."

"You didn't know you were riding with a master navigator. I put a waymark in the GPS at the hotel, and it's recording our track now. We'll get back."

As I spoke, we accidently got funneled off the expressway into Panama City's El Chorrillo District. Here, the American Army had bombed the old, impoverished Spanish neighborhood during the 1989 invasion, letting it burn. The gutted District was a major scar on America's reputation and the operation. Dozens of international organizations subsequently waged protests and lawsuits claiming the United States had used excessive and indiscriminate force. Nobody knows the actual casualties. Estimates range from less than fifty to three thousand.

In the modern computer-generated information age of the first world, we seem to often forget what a military operation really is. It's not a football game. I guess your opinion is based on what side of the line you're on, or who your son fought for. Dean and I had once been on a side of this stark line. We knew well the consequences and benefits of American overkill.

A rough, unsafe no-man's land in the decade after the invasion, El Chorrillo appeared to be recovering, many of the buildings rebuilt. I saw no overt poverty. Still, the District isn't the safest place in Latin America. I quickly drove back under the expressway, disregarding the GPS and motored along a busy, four-lane road until I got back on the expressway, this time paying more attention to the abundant signs pointing the way to the Canal.

• • •

Before viewing the locks, we drove up to Gatun Lake through the Canal Zone and by the plazas of grand official buildings, symmetrically laid out, all with white walls and red clay roofs, and surrounded by parade grounds that gave a hint to the area's ninety years as a US military installation. It all announced a sense of order, something odd in Central America.

We stopped to get a view of the Culebra Cut, once called the Gaillard Cut after Lieutenant Colonel David DuBose Gaillard, the

American engineer in charge of the canal's construction. In 2000, I guess in an attempt to remove some of the Americanization from the canal, the name was changed. Culebra is the mountain range the canal surmounts. So much for the men and machines that carved the passage from the thick jungle.

The cut is a working monument to man's dominance of time and space, an 800-foot wide, manmade valley traversing the continental divide. Here, the eight-mile passageway lowered the mountains from 210 feet to 39, the dynamite and steam shovels removing more than one hundred million cubic yards of earth.

We tried to get a picture at the Pedro Miguel Locks, but were run off by some security guards. Approaching Gamboa, a small town housing canal workers, we were forced to cross a quarter-mile, one-lane, rickety old wooden bridge with a red light that allowed only one-way traffic.

The long, narrow bridge had a pair of three-foot-wide planks sitting a foot above a wooden deck. As we bounced over the loose boards, fear of disaster filled my mind. If we slipped off the three-foot wide path, with the car's limited clearance, at best, we'd get stuck on the deck. The bridge would have to be closed, and a tow truck summoned to rescue us.

The Model S, almost every legitimate consumer advocate's Car of the Year for 2013, had gotten very little negative press, but what negative press it did receive related to several fires that occurred when the battery pack at the bottom of the car collided forcefully with something. The concern was extremely overhyped. Hundreds, if not thousands of gas-burning cars catch fire every year. In the Model S, there is a safety plate below the floor to ensure that any fire, though rare, never reaches the cab.

But bumping over the wooden bridge, soaked with creosote for no telling how many decades, the thought did occur to me. A fire here would not just burn up the car, but likely the bridge too. Even now we'd only be home free when we got on that plane tomorrow, and when the car got back to the States, whenever that would be.

We took a few good pictures, including one at a big sign for the canal, and several with grand ships in the background before stopping at the Mira Flores Locks and Canal Museum. The crowd was enormous, sightseers from every continent. I'd visited these locks before, but due to the growth in the canal's popularity, a new museum and visitors' center had been constructed since.

The museum tells the story of the canal's amazing construction, ten years in all, and costing the lives of 5,600 workers. The French had failed in bridging the seas a decade earlier, but here, the American nation announced to the world that we had arrived. The construction project had many additional benefits—not just the development of new construction technologies, but also aiding significantly in the world's knowledge of how to combat tropical diseases.

From the museum's top deck, tourists can view ships transiting from sea to shining sea, and also gaze on the new locks under construction that will more than double the canal's capacity and size of ships it can accommodate. The new locks will also finally allow maintenance on the three sets of existing locks, in operation almost continuously for one hundred years.

• • •

I've always been astonished by the setting. What egos, if not pure arrogance, the men and young nation must have had to attempt such a massive undertaking in such a desolate, hostile locale.

We Americans don't build things like this anymore. We can barely keep our own roads patched up. There are no more Hoover

Dams, Central Parks, or Golden Gate Bridges on the docket. It's not because we don't love them. I mean everybody, from the new immigrant to Donald Trump, loves this stuff. The crowd around me testifies to that. I myself felt proud, a little conceited. My country and engineers like me built this marvel that's now filling their faces with awe and admiration.

We've been brainwashed by the government—told it is better for them to spend our money taking care of us, and hence, making us dependent on them. Sadly, the days of America triumphantly leading the world to the moon, purely as a symbol that our system is better than yours, that free people can do anything, are gone. Our instinctive desire to go or do because it's fun, what we want to do, human nature—our love of the impossible has been stolen from us. Something like this canal, or the Apollo program, would now be considered government waste, better spent on more pressing domestic issues.

We got here without a drop of gasoline. I'm glad Elon Musk and the other wonderful engineers, scientists, and dreamers at Tesla haven't bought into the dependence mentality.

Sitting on the museum's top deck, I looked at the jungle, reflecting on the trip. Above all odds, we had made it. Feeling almost in a dizzy state, it seemed surreal. What a testament to our perseverance and sheer boldness. It had been special, fun, exciting, more difficult than I'd ever imagined, and always in doubt.

The days, though long, had flown by too quickly, sometimes feeling like the carelessness of a high-school summer. Though often worried, I rarely felt a sense of dislocation. Instead of being harassed by thugs, we were most often saved by the kindness of strangers. As far as I was concerned, we could have gone on forever.

But tempering the joy was the knowledge that this trip was finite, a momentary anomaly from my fate. The feeling of freedom could never last. In a second, I'd turn around and drive back, if life were only that simple and easy. And the little car that now amazed the world would have loved nothing more than to do it again.

Already, my transient ecstasy had begun to fade, the urgent need to get home starting to rule my psyche. My mind danced with the daunting list of things that needed to be done back in the States, stacking up in my brain like a pile of papers on my desk. Begrudgingly, I had to return to the first-world life of capitalism and comforts that most of the world craves, and again start the mind-numbing, daily tasks that prop up that world.

• • •

In some ways, the coming days would be simpler. How easy it's going to be to drive a half-mile down the street and fill up with gas when I need to go somewhere. There'll be no cows in the road to worry about, and generally, everybody will drive on the correct side of the street. I won't have to constantly scan my mirrors for disreputable characters. Lunch and dinner will be easy. I'll order out what I want. My days of freely smoking cigarettes are over. That may be a good thing.

Of course, there'll be the rules, the social norms, the rigid schedules, the meetings, and the punctuality of everything. And the family.

A part of me was already starting to yearn for the friendly Southern accents, the steamy, damp air, the inviting smell of the verdant pines, oaks, and cypresses, the wonderful panorama of miles of cotton and sugarcane, and frogs and insects belching and buzzing around the black water of the bayous and rivers of Louisiana. Those are a part of me as much as I belong to them. I can't help that, and never want to change it.

As only traveling can do, the trip had taken me to a faraway, foreign place—a human delight that never ends. The words of the twentieth-century Pulitzer Prize-winning poet, W. H. Auden, ring as true today as ever:

Man needs escape as he needs food and deep sleep.

At least for now, I felt content, my tormented soul at peace. Hopefully, in a month, or a year or two, I won't be itching to be as far from my life as possible, but I was already starting to ponder the viability of bringing the car back to South America to drive it on to the bottom of the world.

Postscript

The weeks that followed our return to Louisiana were as hectic as the trip, and included a few more days of press. *Motor Trend, AutoWeek, Hybridcars.com,* and several other outlets did stories, and I did a few interviews. The car didn't return to the States for forty-six days. I'll admit, on more than one occasion I wondered if it was actually on a ship somewhere between Panama City and Houston, or driving around Bogotá.

Worries were amplified by the fact that my insurance had expired while the car was in Panamanian customs. I asked the shipping company about insurance, 2.5 percent of the value! After traversing Central America, being "self–insured" didn't seem that radical. But the car finally arrived, safe and sound.

I didn't have a cigarette for a month, my immediate daily problems not inducing any urge. Obviously, this doesn't include the Mardi Gras parades. That's kind of like Central America anyway, everyone leaving us alone for a few weeks, at least for now. Even in the Bible Belt, the open-container laws are suspended and the jails closed to all but murderers and rapists so the well-to-do can stumble around like drunk college kids.

In no time, my days were again filled with too much to do. It took a few weeks for me to stop flinching and cringing when my cell phone would incessantly chirp that hideous sound to tell me somebody needed something. Or Gwen, at the front desk of our office, would break my thoughts and buzz me.

"Randy, can you take a call?"

It was as if she interrupted a funeral.

But I have to keep up with the Joneses in case I ever do end up with the 2.2 kids and a high-maintenance wife. Should we have stopped at that organic campground in Costa Rica? There, I might have found it all, a future family with few needs who'd let me roam.

A few people inquired: "Why go on a vacation like that, constantly on the move? How do you get to truly experience and know the places you've visited?"

What folly and naiveté. What do you learn on the typical week-long vacation filled with guided tours? A much better education comes from driving the open road. Seeing the land. Haggling with natives, bureaucrats, or machine-gun toting *policía*. Watching locals pitch in and help when not paid to, or facing the daily trials and tribulations the citizens endure every day, be it traversing a derelict rural road or experiencing the delight of discovering the cop who just stopped you on an isolated stretch of road is not a crook.

• • •

Though they had numerous requests from media outlets, Tesla never made a formal statement about our trip. This didn't bother me at all. Doing the trip autonomously and without corporate support or acknowledgement added to its glory—the fewer resources, the better. With enough money and support, you can get an electric car to the moon.

I'm still a big fan of the company. I actually can't blame Tesla for not promoting our trip. Its car is designed to motor around suburbia, and it's a wonderful machine to do that. From the company's standpoint, having dozens, if not hundreds, of rednecks and hillbillies, especially ones not as technical or careful as we were, thinking it's cool to motor off into the wild in their electric car is probably a bad idea. Accomplishing what we did is likely the exception, not the rule.

My elation with everything was dampened a few days after our safe return with the news of a pair of Americans that had come up missing in northern Mexico during the same week we passed through the area.

Harry Devert, a thirty-two-year-old investment trader who'd quit his job in New York to drive his motorcycle down to Brazil for the World Cup on a grand adventure, had come up missing in the Mexican State of Michoacán. Tragically, there was not a happy ending to this story, but unlike most south of the border, there was at least some closure. Largely due to the brave and unrelenting efforts of Harry's mom, Ann, the story was widely covered in both the Mexican and American press. Six months after his disappearance, Harry's body was found dumped on a rural plot in plastic bags. What little information has surfaced suggests he was likely a victim of the cartels. Traveling through a small, out-of-the-way town, he may have been falsely mistaken for someone else.

The second was James Robert Stacy who disappeared on a rural road about one hundred miles south of the Texas border as he drove home after visiting his girlfriend in San Louis Potosi. His last communication was with a friend by cell phone, "I'm being followed by two white trucks with armed men and I'm scared." James's bank account was subsequently drained using his ATM card, but his whereabouts are still unknown. Our thoughts and prayers are with James's family. Hopefully, he'll surface.

In fact, it wasn't a good year for Americans in Mexico. In 2014, more than two hundred gringos were kidnapped, almost half in the border region south of Texas—an unfathomable number when you consider the tiny number of Americans dumb enough to brave the area.

But we were very lucky—the gods of fortune had shined on us. Harry and James's heartbreaking stories remind me of the magnitude of our accomplishment. And my satisfaction with our trip still thrills me daily. In my bathroom, I have a list of quotes on the wall that my mother gave me. One is by H. Jackson Brown, an advertising agent who wrote *Life's Little Instruction Book*:

> Be bold and courageous. When you look back on your life, you'll regret the things you didn't do more than the things you did.

I also have a book on my desk by Sonny Barger, the legendary biker and Hell's Angel, titled, *Freedom*. Sonny is likely at the other end of the social stratum from Mr. Brown. I've never read the book. Somebody gave it to me, but it has one of his quotes on the back cover that I love. Seems we all have a few things in common:

> Customize yourself. Originals don't come off an assembly line.